Princess Geek

Dad and daughter,

Braving the new geek chic together

By Lance Arthur Smith, Scottie's Dad

AMAZING SHOWCASE #154 PUBS

BARSOOM • MACONDO • KEYSTONE CITY

Amazing Showcase #154 pubs
a division of Amazing Showcase #154

Cover and layout by John Shartzer
Author photo by Season Bowers

Princess Geek: Paperback edition
ISBN-13: 978-0615845791
ISBN-10: 0615845797

For Scottie

TABLE OF CONTENTS

"It's your kids, Marty. Something's gotta be done about your *kids*."

-Doctor Emmett Brown

Introduction: The Princess Geek

Bedtime for our three-year-old daughter Scottie (her full name is Carmen Scotland Smith) lays roughly between 8 and 9. Earlier this week, Colleen and I relieved our stalwart babysitter around 11 PM, having both put in a long workday. We're married actors, and are fortunate enough to be not only in the same Coronado, CA based company (Lamb's Players Theatre or LPT, for those into the soul of wit), but also in the same production this season. Unfortunately our performances force us to return home well after everyone in the neighborhood has brought in their garbage bins. We like to decompress nightly by watching *Modern Family* or the latest serialized action/drama/high-concept television show. Twenty-two minutes, then off to sleep.

This particular night, as we ambled into bed we heard a tentative little cough, the creaks of failed attempts at opening a door, the titter-tatter of feet across our hardwood floor, another series of attempts to open our door, and finally our daughter's firm request: "we watch Back to da Future?" She does this at least one or two times a week, one of the by-products of moving her out of her crib and into a big-girl (toddler) bed. We acquiesced, and despite it being an ungodly hour for my little weewok to be awake, we relished it. She hoisted her little body, along with her mass of blankets, up into our all-too-tiny queen bed. Smack dab in-between us, she pointed to the screen, asked for *Back to the Future Part III* ("da one with cowboy Marty"), and tucked in for the long haul. 11 o'clock at night. And we let her get away with it. For twenty minutes. That's when we tried to get her back to her bed, and it's also when the walls shook and the heavens raged in our house.

Other evenings she's asked for *Big Trouble in Little China*, *Spider-Man 1* and *2* (I'm reluctant to introduce her to the mess of the third film), *The Twilight Zone*, and *Elmo's Potty Time*, among many others. This assortment of viewing options is not exclusive to bedtime; on the contrary, you never know if she'll choose something "geeky" or "norm". I'll get to those terms in the first chapter. In the meantime, allow me to fill in the rest of the panel (comic book reference).

Colleen and I found out we were pregnant during rehearsals of the musical *Hello Dolly!* The stereotypical exclamation point at the end of the title is indeed courtesy of the musical's authors, and is not my embellishment (I love this show, by the way. And parentheses, as you'll discover the deeper you plunge into this tome). Colleen challenged herself as the choreographer, and it was yet another show where we were cast as romantic leads. At the time, Scottie was not Scottie. She was Botard.

At the end of *Dolly*, a repairman appears to fix the proprietor's roof or something. Our costume designer is incredible- she had also

10

picked coveralls for the actor that sported a nametag: BOTARD. Colleen and I borrowed the moniker to refer to our tiny fetus- this gave it a tangibility. Though we had yet to discover its sex, it now had a name.

In the months that followed, and despite the whirlwind of activities and planning, we found time to imagine what this little person would be like. While finding the baby's heartbeat at office visits (with *some* assistance from the Doc) and likening the infernal device to a tricorder from *Star Trek*, I pondered how much I'd let pop culture and media seep into our weewok's life. My buddy's son coined "Weewok" when he was around three or four. That illustrates my past and ongoing conundrum perfectly- of course I'd let her (we couldn't wait till birth to discover 'it' was a 'she') watch, read, and listen to certain things, but what would those things be? I had a lot of concrete opinions about the issue, and so did my wife. But the concrete opinions mutated into malleable, silly-putty thoughts on a daily, or even hourly, basis.

My daughter's taking her nap right now, which happens to be one of my two optimal times to write (the other is Monday night after 8:30 or so- it's our one day off, Scottie's in bed, and Colleen is at school learning to be a Master of Nonprofit Management). I survey the evidence of today's grandiose adventures: papers strewn about, toys everywhere, crumbs of chicken nuggets and PB&J sandwich on the piano, and trampled crayons. I clean up before my writing session- there's Thor's hammer. She wanted me to fly her around while she summoned the winds to carry her through the clouds. Strapped to her left arm was Captain America's shield, and her uniform of choice- a Tinkerbell outfit, complete with fairy wings. "I go to da fairy meeting, Dada." "Of course," I replied. Why wouldn't you want the added security of the God of Thunder and the Star-Spangled Avenger when traveling to the sketchy dens of Pixie Hollow?

Ah! Here's my *Collected Works of Shakespeare*. It's a heavy, hernia-inducing book with Scottie's favorite Shakespearean character: Bottom, from *A Midsummer Night's Dream*. I find it underneath the Cincinnati Bengals banner hanging in our living room. Scottie watches football with me, but her favorite sports appear to be baseball, fencing, and dancing (dancing *is* a sport).

It's not all cheery, as you most certainly know firsthand. She bypassed the terrible twos and proceeded to the Tharkian threes (Tharks being the war-mongering race of Martians from Edgar Rice Burroughs' *John Carter* series). Timeouts are especially tricky because Scottie might decide to turn the timeout corner into her "dragon castle", where a doorknob becomes a parapet and the wall her Spider-Man scaling slope. Enforcing the rules is constantly an exercise in creativity.

I aim to raise a well-rounded young woman. That's where I'm writing from for the duration of our time together. Yes, there is a great glob of geek in her, but also a healthy helping of everything else a little person needs to become... a big person.

So if you're a single mom with a little boy, will this book be of any use to you? I emphatically reply, "*Yes. I hope.*" Keep in mind that most men are still little boys deep down. Myself included. Boys and girls are becoming increasingly aware of each other's toys and interests (more on that later). If you have no kids, why read? Perhaps my daughter's exploits will resonate with something in your own geeky past. It's cool. If you're not into comic books or movies, or sports, will you understand? Perfectly well, I believe. You're geeky about something, I guarantee.

Thanks for picking up this book. Good luck to both of us. Especially if your daughter is anything like mine, and you are anything like me. You know- **geeky**.

1: Denotation and Connotation of "Geek"

What is a geek?

Geeks. Dorks. Nerds. There are many other synonyms in the nomenclature, but let's look at these three terms.

The official place for hip definitions is urbandictionary.com, and what a place it is- rife with vulgarities, grammatical errors, and dubious contributors. It's also quite stellar. Some of the 319 definitions of "nerd" include "a four-letter word but a six-figure income" and "someone with more knowledge about the computer than the average schmuck." Meanwhile a "dork" can be "abnormally bad at sports and social interaction" and "someone who sits in a tub, farts, then tries to eat the bubbles". While I have never heard of the last one, I'm well acquainted with the majority of the definitions, having been called every variation (including geek) during my school tenure.

Among all the internet searches I conducted, dorks and nerds bordered on pariahs, terms that nobody wants to be known by or with whom they'd like to be associated.

That brings us to "geek". For this one, I pulled out my fifth grade Random House College Dictionary, which bears the inscription "Presented to Lance Smith, Collet Park Spelling Bee Champion 1988" (I faltered in the city trials on the word 'infinitesimal', I believe). Two definitions: 1. A carnival performer who performs sensationally morbid or disgusting acts, as biting off the head of a live chicken. 2. Person; fellow. [probable variation of Scot *geck* meaning 'fool'.]

Again consulting the internet, I found a further proliferation of derogatory ideas of a geek: "a person unhealthily devoted to the pursuit of a singular interest," one who "knows too much for her own good" and "a nerd, just with glasses."

Forget all that. **Geeks are now cool**. It's odd but remarkably true. Consider: Best Buy's "Geek Squad", *Beauty and the Geek* (a TV show I never watched) and "geek chic", whose practitioners generally sport the thick-rimmed black glasses once considered, well, geeky. Websites like thinkgeek.com promote "stuff for smart masses", all while enjoying a heightened public awareness of geek icons the like of Conan O'Brien, Zachary Quinto, and the hottest geek girl from my childhood, Winnie Cooper a.k.a. Danica McKellar (who, by the way, graduated summa cum laude from UCLA's Mathematics Department). Danica is hotter now than she ever was to my 8-year old eyes, but the lust is removed by the realization that she's somebody's daughter. My pal Greg says "having a daughter ruins porn for you". Hm. Having a daughter has certainly shifted me from seeing an attractive woman wearing a scanty outfit (ho-wear) and thinking "why can't I avert my eyes?" to thinking "if my daughter ever wears an outfit like that, I'm telling her to put on a potato sack and swear off dating until I'm ready for grandkids." By the way, I'm appalled by the way girls dress nowadays. Especially on Halloween. When I lived in downtown San Diego (after Scottie was born) I pulled up to wait for the gate to our underground parking and found myself checking out a group of ladies attired… how shall we say… inappropriately. I admired them only for a second, and thought about the stern lecture they'd receive were I their father. One of them was dressed like a slutty Batgirl, but I gave her only minimal notice. I swear.

Most people with whom I've spoken use the term 'geek' when describing a hobby or interest. "I'm such a classic car geek" exited the lips of one of the manliest and hairiest men I know. I geek out over a properly mixed cherry limeade. It used to be that computers, books, and scholarly pursuits were geeky. The geek spectrum has now broadened limitlessly.

***

Many things that used to be cool are now geeky, and vice versa.

In fact geek things are so chic, that sports are almost geeky. Not only do sports fans (I count myself among their number- Go Bengals!) dress up in ridiculous outfits/body paint (Cosplay), they have the temerity to participate in role-playing games honorably referred to as "Fantasy Sports" (yep- I do that too).

By now you've probably heard of Fantasy Sports. You may have a loved one who participates. Let's assume you have no idea what it is. In the simplest terms, using an online management program (or pen, paper, and calculator like my older brother Mark used to do) you pick players to fill out your superteam. Yes, it's a superteam- a veritable JLA (Justice League of Athletes). Based on each athlete's stats, you're awarded points after each game, and guess what? The one with the most points wins. Is there strategy? Die-hards will claim there is. They pore over years of stat sheets, expert predictions, and even trends versus upcoming opponents to set each week's lineups in the hope of making it to their league's championship. Sound familiar? It's Dungeons and Dragons, Gurps, and Heroclix. Role-playing games.

With the roll of a role-playing game's glow-in-the dark D16 (I had one or eight), you have minimal sway in the game's outcome. It's left to chance. Creativity and skill heavily come into play, but chance prevails. Your barbarian's mighty axe may miss cleaving the mage in twain if you roll less than a four. With fantasy sports, chance, and luck more so, reign supreme. "Coaches" talk in terms of "we" when referring to their teams, as if they were on the field with the players gritting their teeth on a crucial 4th and goal from the one-inch line. But if Tom Brady decides to throw three interceptions in a game, it's not as if you can bench him for Aaron Rodgers. Say… now there's a thought. Real-time substitutions based on how well your player performs. CBS Sports, I'll run you through the design if you give me the draft kit for free (including the festive poster with all the neat player stickers). Or even trading cards.

Baseball card collecting was something every red-blooded American boy did, or so went the perception. I had my 80s Oakland A's Jose Canseco and Mark McGwire Donruss cards, my Rickey Henderson and Will Clark Topps cards, but the prize of my collection was my Bill Ripken, Jr. error card by Fleer. Error cards are rare, because they're usually recalled by the distributor and corrected. Errors include wrong jersey numbers, typos in the text, or other bizarre traits. Though elusive, Mark managed to track down the Ripkin card. He's currently a sports editor for our hometown paper, but at the time he was a sportscaster on our local TV station. I don't know if any of this assisted him in finding it, nor do I think I ever got the story. There was always a story; there was no Ebay, no Amazon. You had to go *through* something to get something. At the time I didn't care for my brother's story. There in my grubby paws was Billy Ripkin, hoisting his bat on his shoulder, its pommel visible. Scrawled on the bottom: FUCK FACE. (I'm allowed to use that word once and still get a PG rating, if the classic film *Big* is any indication- Billy asks Josh "who the f*ck do you think you are?" There's also the part where Tom Hanks touches Elizabeth Perkins' boobs, but that's another matter.) Supposedly this "slipped by" Fleer's editors, but

18

this "mistake" made the company a ton of cash and created buzz around its waning sales. They even issued several corrections, each of which proved highly collectible. I remember having one with the text scratched out, one with white out on the pommel, and another sporting a black box. The joys of amassing a ton of collectible crap.

In full geek fashion, we even made our own baseball cards, called Fun Cards. You'd snip the heads out of cards and paste them onto another card. Perhaps you'd even fashion a comic strip-style word balloon with some shenanigans written on it. We thought it was hilarious, especially when using players nobody knew. I remember cutting the head off a hockey guy and pasting it onto a football card while my buddy and I watched another geeky sporting event- *American Gladiators*. Ah, sports.

Being from Albuquerque, we didn't have a pro baseball team, so I could root for whomever I wished. Will Clark's San Francisco Giants were my choice, a decision that was lambasted by my classmates (one of 'em, Walter, even tried to steal my dirty white Giants ball cap). Our Triple-A team was The Albuquerque Dukes (now the Isotopes, which shows the further permeation of geek culture into the mainstream. The Isotopes are Springfield's minor league team in *The Simpsons)*. The Dukes were the farm team for the Dodgers, so I enjoyed the Dodgers and the many players we contributed to them: Mike Piazza or Orel Hershiser were probably the most famous. Sid Bream was another favorite, who went on to play for the Padres. Triple-A ball was fantastic, because the owners were arguably more aggressive than major league teams in creating giveaway days and special events. Meeting Hall-of-Fame pitcher Bob Feller topped Dad's highlights, and he was impressive, but for me one character bested any player- The San Diego Chicken. Along with an Aunt from San Diego, the multi-colored Chicken really got me into the Padres.

When Mom and my stepfather (Pops, hereafter) moved to Las Vegas the AAA team there was the Stars (the farm team for the Padres) and outings with my little brothers always yielded Stars swag. I invested in Minor League trading cards, and waited on the third base side for signatures from the likes of Andy Benes, Sandy Alomar, Jr, Roberto Alomar, and many other Alomars. The players were gregarious, and even hoisted kids dangerously over the side and onto the field to participate in equally dangerous games of catch. I'd later attend Padres games, and took joy in AC/DC's "Hell's Bells" blasting out through Petco Park. This heralded the arrival of star closer Trevor Hoffman (yet another good one the Padres let slip through their fingers- sigh).

Geeks are often criticized for their adherence to rituals, and their single-minded pursuit of passion. Sports geeks are no different. While in college, my roommates and I displayed this obsession in the form of hockey fanaticism. We banged on the glass while watching the New Mexico Scorpions start fights, and cheered as the melting ice swallowed players' skates (it is <u>New Mexico</u> hockey, after all). The Scorpions were terrible, but they were ours. I would come home from classes and rehearsals to watch an evening of hockey on ESPN 2 (those were the days of only two ESPN channels, kids). And once a week our street hockey team, the Hong Kong Goblins, would take to the blacktop. So devoted were we, that we had shirts made up designed by our defenseman (or forward, or wing…) Phil. Some of our shirts even denoted the practice squad subdivision of the Men in Black (we all worked at a movie theatre and sported MIB swag). On our Playstation One, we'd hook up a multi-tap and five of us would check with Chelios in NHL versions '95 through '99. Hockey fans. Hockey geeks. It was cool to like Hockey, which at the time was considered a "fringe" sport. It was mysterious and tough. And totally geeky. The roomies and I would set down the hockey sticks (and joysticks) for another game of skill: poker.

Poker geeks abound. They're still on the edge of geek chic, though it was really post-*Rounders* through 2005 that they were as cool as ReRun. Poker pros will dazzle you with their "math", their precognition, and their ability to "read" one another. Celebrity Poker tournaments let us continue our unhealthy love affair with the rich and famous on our television sets; we con ourselves into thinking that we have *The Right Stuff* (a film Scottie loves, by the way) to take on Tobey Maguire. I love poker. But let's have no illusions about what's going on-you're playing a card game. You might as well be betting on *Go Fish*, though I will admit my amusement at the acting master class that comes into play when anticipating the River. Eyebrow raises, blank faces, or shifty glances tell all. Or not. But it's fun to pretend.

And what is the whole point of getting together to play poker? In my experience, it's to see friends and gab about geeky things: basketball, *Star Wars*, and (occasionally when someone imbibes enough) the music scene.

My own musical tastes run eclectic, and I'm nowhere near as musically geeky as my friend who works at Amoeba Music, but I do consider myself a connoisseur of jazz, classic rock (which is now bizarrely but inevitably considered anything pre-1985), and motion picture scores. Michael Giacchino (*The Incredibles*, *Up*, *Cloverfield*, *Star Trek*), one of my new favorite composers, embodies the hip attitude toward geekdom- liking his stuff and being able to identify recurring themes makes one pretty cool.

Music geeks also contain the subset of record collectors. Mark had an impressive vinyl collection, which made him the coolest guy around then and still shows he's got what it takes to rank in the upper echelon of music geekdom. The man certainly knows his music and the media on which it's contained, and I have vivid memories of being scolded when inspecting his FRAMPTON COMES ALIVE album. Will the next generation even know what records are? My daughter will, I hope. But why is that important to me? Isn't it better to be able to have a fully immersive digital book than the Hardee's kids meal *Gremlins* storybooks I owned as a lad? Different times. I'm split between the tangibility of a book versus the digital imprint of an e-book. Ray Bradbury railed against digital media, yet the availability of his library electronically has led a new generation to discover the imaginative worlds he created.

The way in which we obtain our geeky media is geeky. Even the crotchety, anti-technology Pops knows how to download a movie or share a file using a zip drive- though he still struggles with the very concept of "the cloud." We're so accustomed to using itunes or Amazon to download digital content, not to mention streaming media via Netflix, that we don't stop to consider how geeky we've become. I attribute it to the user-friendly aspect of our technology. My daughter (admittedly a brilliant, future Nobel Laureate) uses our iphones and computers with ease. At three. Many printers now come with a touch screen interface and connect wirelessly to your device for ease of function. Mouses (mice?) have been replaced by track pads, which in turn have morphed into touch screens. Despite the complexities of programs like Pro Tools or

Photoshop, subsequent versions appear to be getting simpler to use. Everyone can be a geek for a minimum of cost and effort. Joy!

In order to circumnavigate confusion over the term "geek", we'll abide by this simple rule: when talking about the past, geek means "very uncool". When talking about now/recent years, geek equates to "James Bond meets Dave Grohl" (which to me is cool).

With the potential for every normal, well-adjusted person to exhibit geeky traits in such a wide variety of disciplines, is it any wonder we're producing more and more geek children?

2: The 80s Child

Why I am who I am, and what my daughter could become. Oh dear.

I recently saw the cover of an Entertainment Weekly, featuring the lineup (badly Photoshopped) of Marvel Studios' *The Avengers*. Time travel to my 13-year-old self, show him the cover, and he'd never believe it. Earth's Mightiest Heroes assembled in one film? My head would've exploded like the escaping convicts in *The Running Man*. The best comic book movies of my time were Richard Donner's *Superman* in 1978 and Tim Burton's *Batman* in 1989. That was pretty much it, and we were lucky to get those and their sequels.

That child of the 80s was born in 1977, the year of *Star Wars*, and existed in a life of pop culture inundation undreamed of by my parents. The Jacksons' Victory tour was advertised on Pepsi cans, MTV actually played music videos (shock!), and with the films of Lucas and Spielberg came the lucrative practice of cross-promotion. Kids in the 80s had an incredible amount of options. We spent our allowance and lunch money on products as straightforward as *ET: The Extra Terrestrial* trading cards, and as ubiquitous as Garfield plush toys with suction cups on the paws (I was quite adamant that Dad's Ford Escort with trendy spoiler sport one of these). Every time we'd chomp down on some delicious McNuggets (packaged in a Styrofoam container) we'd invariably play with our *Transformers* or *Alf* toys included in the Happy Meal. Fast food chains offered premium items like Burger King's *Star Wars* glass line (which Colleen bought me as a Christmas present three years ago) and the McDonald's Muppet glasses (which I bought her last year). We enacted daring scenarios for our *Masters of the Universe* figures out on the playground, with blades of grass and mounds of dirt serving as Eternia's mystic realms. And we read Big Little books; illustrated treasure tomes containing stories of Hulk as he's transported back to the Cretaceous period, or of Donald Duck's latest shenanigans complete with bonus flip book. Granted Big Little Books had been around since the 30s, but this new iteration featured *our* heroes and villains.

To the best of my memory, there was a certain age where all of this was non-geeky and merely chalked up to "kids being kids." The cut-off seemed to rest around 7 or 8 years old. Transformers and GI Joe lasted a little later- through at least fifth grade. While I still collected them, I remember overhearing a bully rant about how namby-pamby it was to play with toys in junior high. A fringe group of us discussed our love for Transformers, and how cool it was that the Predacons combined to form Predaking (I liked to think they were derived from Schwarzenegger's *Predator*), but we knew that airing this passion would have serious ramifications in the kid hierarchy of cool. We were geeks, and we knew it.

In the world of my geek friends, I was strange in that I excelled at sports. I'd plunk down quarters to play TI-99/4A games in the computer lab, but only after basketball practice (Dad coached me and okayed the video game time).

I've managed to exist in both the geek and norm worlds since early childhood. There were advantages, sure, but it's difficult being simultaneously accepted and rejected in both arenas. Being as actively involved in sporting endeavors (soccer, basketball, javelin throwing) as artistic (theatre, dance, music) set me up as an odd duck. I'd race off from doing old-age makeup for *And They Dance Real Slow in Jackson* to throwing javelin for the Track & Field team in the Wilson Relays.

Track and Field events, particularly javelin, appealed to me due to Nintendo's button-mashing classic *Track & Field*, and the hype of the 1984 Los Angeles Olympics. I had a red Velcro wallet that sported Sam the Eagle, the Olympic mascot who was slapped on every product from bubble gum to electric dough mixers (I'm not kidding). But the Olympics aren't geeky, right? They represent the pinnacle of human perfection: unity of body, soul, and mind. Practicing your talent for an ungodly amount of hours each day, forsaking the outside world for a singular focus. Aha! Obsessive devotion to a cause, by my reckoning, is geeky.

So there it is. This sums up my connotation of 'geek' during my youth-doing something *outside of* the norm. Escaping the "real world" for the relatively safe world of imagination and introspection. This world could be shared with other like-minded individuals, individuals who linked minds to create their own safe haven of comfort.

Other activities unified my geeky interests, such as staying up past midnight on Friday nights for NBC's *Friday Night Videos*. I remember convincing Dad to let me prolong bedtime to watch the premiere of Huey Lewis and the News' "Doin' it All For My Baby," which blended my love of Huey Lewis and classic Universal monsters. A mighty seven minutes long, it showed Huey as Dr. Frankenstein and the Monster, along with his bass player as a wicked Dracula.

Horror permeated my youth; from television shows like *Tales from the Darkside* and *Monsters*, to PG-13 horror film *The Gate*. Dad, not really a horror fan, took me to see the Stephen King-penned *Creepshow* at my pleading when I was five (not a practice I plan to emulate with Scottie). I remember freaking out at the "Father's Day" segment, which ended with a corpse carrying a cake adorned with the severed head of his granddaughter. I ducked down in my seat, eventually groping about on the floor. When Dad asked what I was doing I told him I was looking for my glasses. "You don't wear glasses," he reminded. My only reply: "I know, but there's gotta be a pair down here somewhere."

***

My "Real World" of the 80s

Every decade has its uneasy moments, times when the world seems on the very brink of destruction. Moral and physical uncertainty colored many times for me in childhood. Oliver North and the Iran/Contra affair, Reagan's attempted assassination, and the Challenger space shuttle disaster were a few of the events that appeared closer than ever to me through the glass of my TV. The news wasn't just something my folks watched; we talked about these happenings at school, with our peers and our teachers. What will happen? Who will be around in the years to come? My relationship with Dad being what it was, we dissected every news story together. Yet through it all, hope prevailed. When it came to my time at home, however, life could seem incredibly dire at times.

Many things, for me, necessitated a retreat into my world of books, comics, movies, and sports. My parents divorced when I was three, and Mom and Pops had primary custody of me. This proved stress inducing for obvious reasons, not the least of which was the fact that my father was my best friend (and would remain so until his death from cancer my first week of college). That's not to say I had a miserable home life- far from it. I was incredibly fortunate, but there was the muck that sometimes goes along with a less-than amicable divorce (on both sides): Dad would call Mom awful names, and since I idolized him, I went along with it. Mom and Pops would do the same, and proceeded to the deep end when I brought home a racquetball (Dad was a state champ, and I started playing when I was four). Mom forbade me from keeping it, calling it an instrument of the devil or some such shenanigans.

As trite as it may be, it was easier to pick up *The Catcher in the Rye* and commiserate with Holden Caulfield than to deal with the "phonies" in my own life. Ironically, it was Dad who first forced me to read the book (a teacher, he'd assign me book reports to supplement my homework). He used to sweep his hair over his baldpate until I told him that Holden referred to hair sweepers as "phonies". Dad immediately stopped sweeping his hair. I was a snot. I look at all the snotty things I did, knowing that Scottie will probably do most of them to me. Dear, oh dear.

Now I love Mom and Pops, always have, but it was a struggle back then. And for as much as I revered my father (the man was mightier than Zeus to me), I can now look at some of the mistakes he made and perceive him in a more balanced light. Perhaps one of those mistakes was buying me an NES. Kidding, slightly.

Man, I spent too many hours on that thing. Sure I read, did homework, played football, and consistently placed in the top three (out of three) in our playground Olympics. But the 8-bit glamour of that console... it was THE thing to have. You have to understand what a radical jump it was to go from an Atari 2600 (which I didn't own- I had to use a kid's whenever I babysat him) to the Nintendo Entertainment System. Instead of nondescript blocks bopping around the screen, Mario and Luigi were now fully fleshed out (albeit in blocky shapes). Nintendo had licenses better than Colecovision's *Smurfs*. Any given day you could fight Shredder with the *Teenage Mutant Ninja Turtles* or aid Mikey in the awesome sequel *Goonies II*. And we can't forget the nifty beep-beep-beep music (recently mimicked wonderfully in the Universal Studios logo of *Scott Pilgrim vs. the World* and in the lands of Disney's *Wreck-It Ralph*).

My love for the NES proved quite a nifty bargaining chip for Dad when it came to my disobedience. Out past my curfew? A B- on a Math test? No Nintendo for a week. No comics for two. And for serious infractions I'd have to stay in my room. I could work out in my room, but no basketball, no football, and no playing with my best friend Ron for days. Ron received similar punishment, yet was much better flaunting authority than I was. He jumped out his first-story window once to defy his parents. However, I pictured him bursting through the glass of the second story like Batman, cape pulled tight around his frame to protect his face from the shards. Dad never pushed me to those extremes, but his form of punishment known as "Restriction" pissed me off incessantly.

Admittedly, I much preferred the Mom and Pops school of punishment. They spanked me, a form of punishment that never did and never will work for me. I inherently disagree with the practice (Dad only spanked me once, when I was five, for throwing our red rotary phone across the room), and it failed to get my folks' desired result- compliance. I learned at an early age that all I had to do was clench my ass and deal with a little sting. I was then free to do whatever I wished. Do something horrendous? Get a spanking for one minute, and then move on with your life. Lesson learned? Naw. I remember getting a spanking for something or other, whipping up some fake tears, running to my room, and turning on the TV to catch the edited version of *The Terminator*. I'd inevitably repeat whatever it was I did wrong. At Dad's, however, I was entirely reluctant to repeat the offending behavior.

Dad had another form of punishment that I intend to duplicate with Scottie (yes, I've come to face the harsh reality that she's gonna screw up). Most minor goofs caused me to furnish my father (an Educator, by trade) with 100-, 200-, or 500-word reports on the infraction. For heavy gaffes, I strained my wrist writing 1000-word reports. If he caught me in a lie (one of the worst offenses in our house) the subject could be a history of deception, or the lies a politician had told.

Still on the writing track, every movie we saw together was

accompanied by a review. Dad paid me a quarter for each review, but it was understood that upon completion of *Spaceballs* or *Predator* it was incumbent on me to explain how Mel Brooks used parody and satire, and how Arnie outsmarted an alien hunter who was physically superior (surely the "wits" he displayed as Dutch helped studios see the intelligent side of Arnold, leading to *Junior* and the note-perfect *Batman and Robin*. Lest sarcasm be lost on the page- that's sarcasm). If you think Dad was the only one with Olympian academic standards, please note that my mother was also a teacher, and had the same "a B doesn't cut it" attitude toward my education.

Dad, Mom, and Pops didn't have much of anything in common, save this: they all loved me. At the core, amidst their fighting, games, and hubris they ultimately put me above all else. That's what parents do, even when they lose sight of it at times.

I spent the rest of my 80s tenure surviving Elementary school, a change of custody from Mom to Dad, the relocation of Mom and Pops (and my little brothers) to Las Vegas, and the transition to Middle School. 6th grade shop class introduced me to the wonders of educational video games, chief among them *Oregon Trail* and *Odell Lake*. I also took a girl to the school dance, though she forced me to do it.

Because of this, I remember having a conversation with Dad about love and marriage somewhere around the time *Married with*

Children was popularizing the Sinatra tune. Dad's advice was flippant and brief.

How did he and Mom meet? It was one of the few times he spoke of Mom with fondness (they met on the grass of a park), and a question that remained unasked of Mom. I'm not entirely sure why I never (and still haven't) asked: perhaps I didn't want to stir the pot, inviting an opportunity for criticism or negativity. From my vantage point, marriage was a burden but parenthood was akin to Indy's quest for the Lost Ark of the Covenant. Mom and Dad (independently of one another) illustrated that being a parent was rewarding, frustrating, and an incredible human experience that not everyone will (or wants to) take. But those that embark on the path are fulfilled in great (though not always apparent) ways. I got it, then. I wasn't hot on getting married, but always wanted to be a father.

Still, I clung to the idea that something wasn't right. Finding a true partner to share the experience of parenthood would surely enrich my life, and that of our child, even more. At twelve I wasn't in any rush, but I couldn't help wondering- what would my future weewok be like?

3: Along Came a Weewok

Colleen and I met under interesting circumstances. I was working in the Sea Lion and Otter show at Sea World (for that story see my forthcoming book, *Mimebeard*), and was married but separated. My wife at the time was in town and we went to a dinner at a hacienda-esque restaurant in Old Town with the cast. Colleen was dating one of my co-workers, and their relationship was nearing an end. One lady, a mermaid in our show, was cheating on her fiancé with someone in the show. Also at the table: another guy who was cheating on his girlfriend, possibly with someone else at the table, and a happily engaged couple (who are still married, I believe). A mess of a situation. But the enchiladas were tasty.

Shortly after this ill-fated evening, my ex and I decided to divorce and I forged ahead with life in San Diego. Almost a year later, Colleen and I became reacquainted during a play reading of *Tiger at the Gates*, a sort of prequel to *The Iliad*. I played Ajax, the hotheaded Greek, and Colleen was Cassandra, resident Trojan crazy. We hit it off, especially when commiserating over our bizarre dinner at the hacienda. Rehearsals went incredibly well, though I could tell you more about Colleen than the script. On my way to the actual reading, a Ford Mustang plowed over my motorcycle and I rolled through the intersection. Mostly uninjured, and instructed by my director to hurry my ass to the theatre (put more kindly, but with the same subtext), I rode my dented bike to the reading. In a deluge. Colleen and I rehearsed our one scene together, drenched and cold as I was. Our moment of stage combat rehearsal ended in Colleen ripping my soggy green sweater. Just prior to the reading, she ran to procure a bandage or ice; she produced neither and the show began. We finished the reading with hugs and such, and we wouldn't see one another for a few more months.

There were several "friend" hangout sessions encompassing dinners, movie marathons, and a heart-wrenching viewing of the original *Superman* movie (I tear up when Ma tells Clark "I know, son… I know"- John Williams' music swells, the camera sweeps up to show Ma and Clark in the field, and glory shines).

I was reluctant to date her, due to the unwritten "guy code" which, unofficially, states: don't date your co-worker's ex-girlfriend. As ludicrous and unreasonable as this may seem, I'd made up my mind that this was the way it was done. My stance changed (a bit) on New Year's Eve. Colleen found out about my stumbling block to our romantic relationship, and came out with a group of us that New Year's Eve to downtown San Diego's Mr. Tiki- a lover's paradise (tagline mine). Everyone was a couple except for us, and the time came for the requisite

New Year's kiss. I kissed her... on the cheek. Then gave the "it's all good, friend" back pat. This elicited the response all desire on New Year's- she stormed off onto the dance floor.

Feeling like a heel, I was presented with a permission slip Colleen jokingly forged from my co-worker. It gave me permission to kiss her, and enjoy it to boot. So I kissed her. For real this time, while something akin to Dee-lite's "Groove is in the Heart" funked up our New Year. We started dating New Year's Day, after I called my co-worker and informed him I planned to date her (he was in complete support).

The DTR (define-the-relationship) happened the day after our first kiss. I've never been the type to date around, though I told Colleen I didn't expect her to be exclusive. Thankfully (because of course I *didn't* want her to date other people) she said she wanted to date only me. This was, in a word, rad.

Having been married before, I knew what I wanted and what I didn't. One night over Chinese food, and just about at the one-year point, I brought up marriage to Colleen (quite casually, now that I think about it). She put down the Kung pao chicken and calmly discussed the marital matter with me. I was as matter-of-fact about the issue as I was about our DTR. I think it was around college when I solidified what I wanted out of a family life: a wife, a kid, and a lawn to mow on Saturday morning. These were not "achieve at all costs" objectives, merely things to which I aspired.

Colleen, with her usual aplomb, responded favorably to this conversation. No definite date was set, no formal proposal. Just an understanding. It was very grown-up of us. We then resumed watching a James Bond movie (*Thunderball*, I think) and settled back into our cream cheese wontons. Very grown-up.

Over the next few months, we talked of children: what we were like as kids, what traits we'd like to see in the next generation. Gently but plainly probing, we figured out we both wanted kids. Score. The proposal manifested on New Year's Eve (one year after we started dating, for those doing the upper-level math). Colleen told me she loved the lady in Old Town who made tortillas on the sidewalk outside of a Mexican restaurant; she loved her so much she wanted to include her in her will.

I decided to contact management and use the engagement ring as a sort of napkin holder (in this case, a tortilla holder). Unaware of my elaborate series of Jack Bauer espionage, Colleen opened her tinfoil to discover the ring and the tiny tortilla. I bent to one knee and popped the question. Her response, which still gives me chills, was "I love the tortilla lady!" Unsure, I asked if that meant that she'd marry me. She replied "Oh yeah, of course!" Thus with teenagers impatiently waiting for their floury butter troughs (and with looks of "oh that's classy"), I kissed my bride-to-be and we made our way out of Old Town newly betrothed.

Many adventures followed during that year, including our wedding, and talk shifted again to children. We were moving into rehearsals for *Hello Dolly!* and while I've spoken to this in the **Introduction** I'll add one final tidbit. I don't know that I've ever felt the sheer terror I experienced nightly (and twice on Saturdays) as I hoisted Colleen toward the lights on one of our many lifts. I've always felt pressure when we danced, both as an actor dancing with the choreographer, and as a husband dancing with his (demanding) wife. Colleen pushes me when she choreographs- it's nerve-wracking but craft strengthening. This paled in comparison to the stress of protecting your wife and baby while hurling them to the heavens. All turned out well in the end, but I was a wreck during this entire sequence.

That wind-up to Scottie's arrival contained many baby showers, given by magnificent friends. Seriously, I had no idea how much effort went into a baby shower, and as floored as I was by our friends' generosity in the past, it couldn't compare to the new level of hospitality they brought when throwing showers. A diaper shower (that's four uses already of the word 'shower'- ain't babies grand?) consisted of small cucumber sandwiches at a quaint and intimate gathering hosted by dear friends Chrissy and Jerry. Indicative of our geek tastes, at another shower we received *Guitar Hero II* for the Playstation 2 (with additional guitar), zoo passes (love them sky buckets!), and a motorcycle gift certificate. The latter was for me, as Colleen never supported my Captain America-esque 1986 Honda Rebel 450. Silver and sporty and, sadly, sold. For the sake of Colleen's sanity and my skin.

Preparation for the baby continued apace. I put the crib together in record time while Colleen endured baby kicks on the couch. That child danced (I like to think she was practicing her sword fighting) inside Colleen's tummy. Or perhaps Scottie's activity was stirred by the fact that *Indiana Jones and the Last Crusade* played boldly on our TV. For the record, I prefer *Raiders*, Colleen prefers *Last Crusade*, and nobody prefers *Crystal Skull*. Nobody.

One week after her due date, Scottie made her presence known during back-to-back viewings of *Phone Booth* and the Harrison Ford starrer *Air Force One*. To this day, I've not taught Scottie the phrase "get off my plane", but once she reads this book I dearly hope she'll add that to her repertoire. Colleen went through contractions all night: I felt utterly useless. The intuitive wife knows how to deal with a dejected husband, and Colleen is indeed an intuitive wife. She demanded I go to bed and if she needed me she'd let me know. I was probably making her trial worse with my dotage. I slept like the dead, and was awakened by Colleen gravely intoning "um, I think it's happening." Fortunately, I had read *The Caveman's Pregnancy Companion* in its entirety, so I knew everything there was to know about everything (err… mostly). With the overnight bag packed, I got Colleen down to the car. And she got down to business.

"I peed my pants." She said this, not me (though I did do a quick inventory of my drawers). I mentioned that this might be her water breaking. "I KNOW WHEN I'VE PEED MYSELF, LANCE!" Choosing not to argue with her, I rushed to get her a sweatshirt on which to sit, and after racing to the hospital she acquiesced that perhaps I was right. Colleen, wanting to appear heroic, also demanded that we eschew the emergency loading zone parking directly in front of the doors (in which they'd told us to park during a hospital tour months before) in favor of the underground parking lot. We pulled into the garage and, of course, the nearest spot was quite far from the doors. A seeming football field in length. Scottie was fast approaching.

I had lugged all our gear halfway when Colleen decided that retreat was the better part of pregnancy valor. We zipped back up the ramp and parked out front. What followed was a blur. Colleen had a fever and her mother, sister, and I had to continuously apply ice-cold washcloths to her. During this time, she mugged for the camera (which she'd initially forbidden, but I brought it figuring she'd change her mind) and used the red-lit hospital switch affixed to her index finger as an *ET: The Extra Terrestrial* reference. She even made me shoot a music video for "Turn on Your Heart Light" which she sang in a bluesy, delirious voice. She closed with "beeeeeee gooooooood" and then decided it was time for the camera to go bye-bye. Scottie, nearing the end of her journey, must have absorbed this last bit of geekdom before her entrance, as one of her earliest and favorite things to do was extend her index finger in greeting while voicing ET's signature command. Scottie has yet to develop a taste for Reese's Pieces, but has asked me to fly her on her tricycle on multiple occasions.

Many icy washcloth sessions later, it was determined the safest way for Scottie to arrive was to come out via Colleen's stomach. We'd not exactly prepared for a C-section, but always knew it might be a possibility. In fact, our pregnancy class was so boring that we ditched the second one- the one dealing with Cesareans.

Briefly separated, we were reunited after I donned hospital scrubs and a groovy hairnet. A sheet was placed across my bride's midsection, and they went to work. The doctors and nurses were fantastic, and Colleen was, well, badass. Things happened rapidly- a push, the whirr of surgical instruments, and I was asked if I wanted to see my kid. I peered over the sheet to see Scottie's head pop OUT OF COLLEEN'S STOMACH. Besides pure elation, it temporarily reminded me of an Alien Chestburster/Kuato hybrid.

Weary but relieved, Colleen managed a smile and I happily

kissed her. The hospital staff walked me over to a sterile table to cut the

cord and inspect my weewok. The most amazing thing to me was the size

of her feet. Froggy feet, we'd later christen them. Gigantic and scaly,

almost Godzillian in retrospect. Scottie seemed to know shenanigans

were afoot, and she wanted no part of them. She didn't really scream; just

kicked and gave everyone the stink-eye. I escorted Scottie to the nursery,

having been told that I'd be able to see Colleen shortly.

She floored 'em in the nursery. The on-duty attendant turned

Scottie on her stomach, but the little tyke used her Play-doh arms to do a

push-up. "She is a warrior!" the attendant exclaimed. Damned skippy, I

thought. She's a regular Ripley or Vasquez.

We finally made our way back to the room, a veritable palace

and something for which we weren't prepared. During the tour they

showed us a place akin to the hall closet in which you keep your Boggle

and fishing rods. Now we were treated to the *Rain Man* suite.

The three of us didn't get much sleep, and my biggest fear was

falling asleep on the cot and crushing Scottie. I didn't sleep when I had

her next to me. Actually, I didn't sleep- ever. It's quite incredible what

the human body can do when the need arises. We had many visitors and I

was grateful for the respite from hospital food when a friend loaded us

up with In N' Out. When we weren't quaking in fear at the prospect of

parenthood, we engaged in one of our favorite activities: movie watching. *Clue* and *When Harry Met Sally* played on our television while we figured out how to change diapers and swaddle our new bundle of joy. Again, is it any wonder Scottie loves movies, when her first few days on the planet were spent watching the small screen?

Perhaps it's time for me to explain the name 'Scottie'. Her full name is Carmen Scotland Smith. Carmen is a family name, given to Colleen's Mom, Grandmother, and Great-Grandmother. Colleen's grandma went by Nan, her mom by Chuchi, and her Great-Grandmother by Momma. We knew we wanted Carmen to be our kiddo's first name too. As fans of *The West Wing*, we wanted to incorporate CJ into her name (after CJ Cregg, natch), so the search was on for a 'J' middle name. I wanted Jordan (after Green Lantern Hal) but Colleen immediately nixed that one. Somewhere in this quest for CJ, a friend of ours went through her list of names with Colleen. She had apparently named all her future children and one of those was Scotland. Colleen latched onto it immediately, and I did too after realizing it would give us a good reason to visit the country, something we didn't do until much later. Carmen Scotland won out, and the nickname "Scottie" became the standard.

I've done my best to describe the hospital affair, but the entire process is a bit hazy to me now. At the time, I was playing the Priest in *The Light in the Piazza* and to this day have difficulty telling you what the show's about. SPOILER! I've since determined it needs more George

Hamilton and less horse kicks to the head. I'd stay at the hospital, except to perform *Piazza*, and we occupied the room for three days. When we left I had two objectives: get my wife AND my daughter home alive. I accomplished both.

The weewok had landed.

4: Pop culture pops up

Movies, Television, and Music

As you've no doubt surmised (and you read the **Introduction**, right?), Scottie comes from a strong pedigree of geekdom. The majority of my formative pop culture years were spent sifting through the 80s. However, the 90s played no small part in my personal Path of Geekdom.

As a fourteen-year-old and a high school freshman in 1991, Nirvana blew my mind. I bought an abundance of flannel shirts at the 50-Off store and one of those flannels, a black and grey John Connor-style, adorned my frame as I (and all my friends) flocked to see Arnie zipping around the LA River on a motorcycle in *T2: Judgment Day*. Now, I grew up listening to Warrant, DJ Jazzy Jeff and the Fresh Prince, and Pearl Jam, but thanks to my father (a product of the Great Depression) I was also into Leon Redbone, Bing Crosby, and other classics.

Michael Jackson factored heavily in my love of performing arts. And the man was indeed an ARTIST. At five, I saved birthday money to buy my first album- Michael Jackson's *Thriller* on cassette tape. MJ was everywhere- you couldn't pick up a Pepsi can without being reminded that you were making "the choice of a new generation." While his popularity had waned for a bit in the 2000s, it skyrocketed with his death and the subsequent release of his rehearsal concert *This Is It*. We haven't pushed him at Scottie, but she latched on to his beats quite young. And recently, she's become obsessed with him. She's got *Beat It* memorized, and is working on the *Bad* album. Just this morning we lay in bed listening to two of the four discs from MJ's Ultimate Collection. And we were completely content. Scottie also uses the full title *Michael Jackson's Moonwalker* when requesting the film. We're all gaga for the King of Pop.

At the time I found it interesting that I was actually one of the popular bunch based on my opinion of the King of Pop. Everyone loved the man. My popularity ended with frequent trips to the Putt-Putt arcade. Playing *Karate Champ* for hours on end does not endear one to the cool kids. But I'd have my day again, and it was all thanks to a little hobbit.

Lord of the Rings not only legitimized geeky things, but it won an Oscar. As I write this, geeks and norms are tweeting and blogging about the trailer for *The Hobbit*. I had the pleasure of reading the LOTR trilogy for the first time while working as an extra on Sam Raimi's *Spider-Man* (I re-read *The Hobbit* while surrounding Billy Bob Thornton and Bruce Willis as an extra in *Bandits*). The cinematic versions of *Spider-Man* and *X-Men* the year before it proved that comic books were a legitimate and lucrative way to whet the public's appetite for stories.

The legitimization of geekdom occurred in the early to middle

2000s on arenas great and small, and we were inundated with images. Pre-hipsters reveled in the glory of *Beat the Geeks*, a game show on Comedy Central which featured contestants matching wits with four geeks: movie, music, television, and guest geek. *Side note- actors in LA tend to do a lot of game shows while waiting for... anything. I went on *Wheel of Fortune* and scored some cash there. On *Beat the Geeks* I managed to beat the James Bond geek, and bested the movie geek in the final round. My winning question? "What animal did Dick van Dyke dance with in the classic film *Mary Poppins*?" If you don't know, I'm sure the person next to you has the answer.

To this day, I'm amazed that one of my favorite indie comics has transformed into a pop culture juggernaut. *The Walking Dead* not only continues AMC network's trend of popular "cutting-edge" entertainment, it smashed cable broadcast records. It's even made the zombie genre hip and cool. I had to re-read that last sentence. Unreal. And I'd wager the vast majority of its viewers don't know the source material, or that it's even based on a comic book.

This brings us to the widespread influence of Disney in the pop culture consciousness. My brothers and I marveled at each new Disney film, ranging from our earliest introduction (*Pinocchio*) to later incarnations on *The Wonderful World of Disney* (itself a new iteration of the anthology tradition begun in the 50s with the *Disneyland* television series). Colleen and I decided early on that TV time for Scottie (and, by proxy, us) would have to be dramatically controlled. One hour max, per day, we thought. That's good. Nothing rated PG or above. We also foolishly decided we wouldn't take her to Disneyland until she reached 5. Thankfully, we rescinded this edict and took an almost one-year-old Scottie to the Tiki Room; the magic of animatronic and slightly malfunctioning birds mystified our girl and, through her eyes, us.

I feel that the TV watching constraints have become negotiable, in either direction, depending on the need and Scottie's age. Bargaining chips, something to which I never thought I'd be beholden, have proven valuable. Most Disney films rated G or even PG are acceptable in most situations. Scottie repeatedly watches a select few (*Newsies*, for instance, provides a welcome dance break in her day), which we love and loathe. Netflix has become our go-to for some time, as we expunged DirecTV from our lives (after last football season, of course). Without network television, we're not pounded with ads for products as much, yet Scottie is as aware of toys as I was. However, we're able to regulate most of it, and even that regulation is mostly unnecessary. The child thankfully doesn't crave toys; she's delighted when she opens a gift to find Tinkerbell and the gang or a talking Captain America, but even walking down the aisles of Target seldom yields a purchase. I can't explain it, since I used to work my wiles on Mom in Costco, and we'd inevitably return with the latest *Teenage Mutant Ninja Turtles* VHS (remember those?).

Other films aren't as innocuous as the turtles. The weewok saw the cover for *Enter the Dragon* and thought it looked cool. I made the mistake of betraying how excited I was at her interest in a Bruce Lee film, which only strengthened her insistence on watching it. I have to fast forward through almost the entire R-rated film, and need to stress the fact that Sammo Hung and Bruce Lee are only "practicing" their moves in the beginning. She'll catch fleeting images as I fast forward, and immediately states "dat's not 'propriate for me." Interestingly, she also uses that term to stand in for something she doesn't want to do. "Pick up your toys, please, Scottie." "I can't, Daddy. Dat's not propriate for me."

Another dangerous DVD box cover is that of *The Shawshank Redemption*. I had to explain that one day, when she's bigger, we could watch Daddy's favorite film together. Scottie's barometer of growth is "when I'm bigger I can ride da Hulk ride" (at Universal Studios' Islands of Adventure). She has since amended that. "When I'm bigger, I can ride da Hulk ride and watch da Shawshank Medention."

Netflix's streaming service provides us with many shows of yesteryear to introduce to our weewok, and a classic that resonates with Scottie is *The Cosby Show*. On constant rotation is the episode where Cliff wants Rudy to play football. Scottie loves it, and cheers for Rudy to "run faster wif da ball, through da kids, to da other side". She also enjoys the episode where Cliff takes the kids to a vaudevillian performance. One of the actors is Bill Irwin, who Scottie recognizes as the new Mr. Noodle (replacing the irreplaceable Michael Jeter). Colleen and I are huge fans of Mr. Irwin, and were delighted to see that his clowning routines brought endless giggles to Scottie; though she was perturbed at one part when she was in the two to two and a half age range. Toward the end of the episode, Bill Irwin invites the kids to "disappear" down into his magic trunk. Scottie would freak out at this part, begging the kids not to go in. Even their reappearance did little to set her at ease. She could always handle peekaboo as an infant and toddler, but it was interesting to note this reaction nearly every time we watched the episode (we offered to turn it off, but she pleaded we keep it going). Since then her interest in Cosby has waned, but it's a show to which I hope we can return. She's currently leaving behind Dr. Huxtable for another of his ilk. Sort of.

***

Hello, Doctor

A trip to Comic-Con usually yields plenty of free bounty, and one of the coolest things I plucked was a sampler DVD of three or four BBC (British Broadcasting Corporation) shows. Amidst a forgettable *Torchwood* and a decent excerpt from *Jekyll* was a little show I'd not seen since I was probably six. That show was *Doctor Who*.

Were I to admit that I watched *Doctor Who* back when it was on our local PBS station, all my fellow kindergarten and first grade pals would surely have scoffed. Geekier than *Star Trek*, it aired on PBS which only added to its geekiness. I grew up with the scarf-wearing Tom Baker incarnation of the Doctor- for the uninitiated, the Doctor has been played by several different actors over the years; unlike James Bond, a new actor is justified by the fact that the Doctor "regenerates" when he's nearing death, and that regeneration requires a new body.

Matt Smith plays the current Doctor, but the previous version (and arguably most beloved in the recent fan community) was embodied in the wild-eyed David Tennant. He's my wife's favorite Doctor, and my second favorite (Christopher Eccleston is my pick). It's still incredible to me that Colleen is an even bigger fan of the show than I am. And she's not geeky about movies in the slightest. But she loves David Tennant. The interesting thing with Tennant is his cross-genre geek appeal. He also appeared in *Harry Potter and the Goblet of Fire* as Barty Crouch, Jr., certainly a lure for fans of that series. On our recent trip to the UK, we managed to procure seats to Tennant and his *Doctor Who* co-star Catherine Tate in Shakespeare's *Much Ado About Nothing*. The theatre was a madhouse. It was completely packed, and absolutely past fire code with standing-room only tickets. Folks waited outside the theatre afterward to meet their geeky, British hero. I smiled. After all, how many of them were brought to Shakespeare through their obsession with *Doctor Who*?

I can't recall exactly how Scottie was introduced to the wonderful world of the Doctor, but I believe it was during one of her attempts to stall bedtime. Such is her desperation to stay awake, that she'll occasionally proclaim, "We watch anyfing, anyfing!" Prior to *Doctor Who*, I was watching the Tyrone Power *Zorro* with her (she had just turned two) and in an effort to circumvent bedtime she slashed the air three times with an imaginary sword, pointed to the screen, and asked, "We watch more Zorro?" Similarly, a week or two later Colleen told her it was bedtime, and on that evening we happened to be watching a David Tennant episode of the Doctor's travels ("The Shakespeare Code" perhaps). Scottie screamed "more *Doctor Who*!" She pushed this phrase so hard that she actually started crying. Colleen and I made one of our famous deals (yes, we shook on it with Scottie) whereby she could stay up for three more minutes, provided she go to bed without a peep. Satisfied, Scottie nuzzled close to Colleen and enjoyed her three minutes of the Doctor's adventures.

One of the most enjoyable aspects of the show is the Doctor's use of "intellect and romance over brute force and cynicism" (to quote Craig Ferguson). The Doctor's only weapon is a sonic screwdriver, a sort of skeleton key that unlocks and reveals the logic behind a problem. He travels in and out of history, past and present, in his blue phone box (the TARDIS: Time And Relative Dimension in Space). If you know *Bill and Ted's Excellent Adventure*, it's similar. Sort of. Sound geeky? It most certainly is. Yet somehow this show has geeked its way into the pantheon of cool. I asked friends in the UK if the good Doctor enjoyed the same level of popularity there as he did here in the States. Nope, they replied. *Exponentially greater*. And if the use of the word 'exponentially' isn't a clue to the geek chic employed overseas, then I'll be a Dalek.

Scottie's most-watched episode is "The Runaway Bride," a nod to her fixation with marriage. While I endorse her interest in the show, I'm not a fan of her constant talk of marriage (more on that in the **Theatricality** chapter, where she married Hudson of "weewok" fame). I can barely deal with the fact that the kid goes to preschool, so rapid is her growth and maturity. Thankfully my own bride reminds me that we have time till that event occurs. Colleen, my coolant when I'm overheating. She's also our household decorator. Our Christmas tree was bathed in blue and white, perfectly matching our tree topper- Colleen's homemade blue TARDIS.

***

Nostalgia

A love and reverence for the past connects everyone, regardless of generation. There's always a generational thread of commonality that exists in the pop culture of the past. *Explorers* was about a group of kids, from different backgrounds, who pooled their talents to build a craft to the stars. I believed I could do this, though certainly not on my own. I'd need my own cadre of like-minded and industrious folks. First recruit was my brother Trampas (named after a character on *The Virginian*; Mom and Pops loved/were geeky about that show). We never attempted constructing the ship, but always talked about that one day when we'd try it. Trampas and I are so different, and he's not really a "movie guy," but get us together now and we could quote *Explorers*. We'd probably even remember the schematics for the spaceship. 80s pop culture bonds us, forever.

And it's like that the world over. Colleen's 80s experience was similar. When asked if there were one movie that encompassed our childhood, and carried all our hopes and dreams, Colleen and I would probably agree on Robert Zemeckis' *Back to the Future*. So would Scottie.

In another one of our "this is how we're gonna parent?" discussions, Colleen and I debated about films like *Back to the Future*, ones that we saw as kids (I was seven) but obviously contained some questionable language and material. I should point out that the antiquated MPAA ratings system seldom plays a part in which programs we deem suitable for our child, as we make it a point to watch a film prior to a

Scottie viewing. We were on the fence with *Back to the Future*, but I was confident she'd appreciate it.

Marty and Doc introduced themselves to our child, in a way. I blame Universal's marketing department for creating such a kick-ass poster design (replicated on the DVD). Marty stands outside the Delorean with his sunglasses flipped up, checking his watch, while fire trails streak past him. Scottie plowed through our DVDs one day, nearly stopping on *Hello Kitty* when the aforementioned Michael J. Fox cover dropped her jaw.

"Dis one." She was one and a half. I said no, saying that it wasn't entirely appropriate for her (as mentioned, she now uses 'appropriate' in the negative; when she's offered a lunch she doesn't want, she huffs "dat's not propriate for me"). She pleaded, and I figured sure. Of course, I forgot to ask Colleen, but later she thought it might be okay. Heh.

Initially, Scottie was uncertain about Marty. After all, he plugged in his guitar and almost blew himself up. But as soon as Doc's voice told Marty that the clocks were slow and Huey Lewis' "Power of Love" kicked in, Scottie's mind was blown. She wanted more. Over the course of the next few days we watched all three films over and over. Scottie memorized the trilogy to the point of wanting specific scenes ("fast forward to when Doc saves da girl on his flying skateboard" or "play dat again where Doc says 'da Libyans!'").

Fearing mimicry, Colleen and I decided to take a hiatus from the movies. There is quite a bit of swearing in them, and some questionable antics. Let's pause and reassess, we agreed. Marty's exploits were put aside, until almost a year later.

Last summer, we were fortunate enough to travel to the UK with our theatre company. It was incredible; my highlight had to be staying in the Highlands of Scotland. We spent the weekend at a small bed and breakfast in Poolewe, on the Northwestern edge of Scotland. I'd look out at the loch while listening to James Horner's sweeping *Braveheart* score. Colleen spent much of our time there sick in bed. As such, I think her highlight of the trip was attending the *Doctor Who Experience* in London. We weren't able to take Scottie, but thankfully Minga (Colleen's mom) stepped in to take care of her at our place. We were gone three weeks, and while it was an incredible journey, it was excruciating to be away from our weewok for so long. As a coping mechanism (I like to believe) Scottie frequently requested the BTTF trilogy. Every day. Minga complied, and soon Scottie (at this point 2 and a half) was spouting dialogue from the films better than some of my 80s contemporaries.

Her familiarity with the films blossomed further, and last Halloween (two weeks after her third birthday) she requested to dress up like Marty McFly for trick-or-treat purposes (that picture is in the beginning of this very book). The year prior we dressed her up as Charlie Chaplin due to her love of the comic genius' films. I admit that was mostly our prodding, though she did enjoy it and even attempted Chaplin's signature strut. Last year, Marty was all her.

So precise are her tastes, her knowledge of the films so intricate, that her request was to dress up like *cowboy* Marty. We thought she meant 'Clint Eastwood' Marty from *BTTF III* in poncho and gunfighter hat. We asked her if this was right and she stomped her feet (yes she does this; not regularly, thank you very much). "I want da cowboy Marty where Doc dresses him up at da movies." Translation: Atomic, 1950s cowboy Marty complete with frill and Nike shoes. At the drive-thru.

We thought this might be a little too obscure, and told her she'd get a hoverboard if she dressed up in the recognizable denim jacket, red puffer vest (life preserver), and red undershirt. She begrudgingly agreed.

Colleen busted out her art skills, and Scottie even scored an authentic cardboard hoverboard, one that zipped over the ground (with a bit of help from Daddy). The weewok remained literally clothed in our nostalgia.

***

Rock on

One of the most recognizable things about *Back to the Future* and its sequels is the distinctly 80s music that we rocked out to on our

Walkmans back in the day. Huey Lewis dominated my playlist. And by playlist, I mean mixtape collection. As mentioned earlier, Dad let me stay up past midnight to watch the popular *Friday Night Videos* and the premiere of Huey Lewis and the News' new video "If This Is It" (I also got to see The Whispers' "Rock Steady" three years later, and I still can't understand how it cracked the 80s pop charts). NBC had FNV. We didn't have cable, and I'd watch MTV only at friends' houses. Once a week from 12:05 AM to 12:35 AM, NBC presented half an hour of videos (which was really 15 min worth of videos after commercials).

Was it a questionable practice for a seven-year-old to stay up past midnight? Perhaps. But it was also something Dad and I shared, although I'm sure I enjoyed the late-night luxury far more than he did. As stated earlier, his tastes ran toward the Mills Brothers, jazz, Howard Keel and such. I always equated Mom with the gospel hymns and Crystal Gayle records and 8-tracks I found lying around the sound deck; it wasn't until later that my intrigue into her formative music years was piqued, having discovered that she was a huge fan of Creedence Clearwater Revival. CCR? Now *that* I could get behind.

Despite me jamming to tunes like Young MC's "Bust a Move" and Paula Abdul's "Cold-Hearted Snake" while roller-skating in PE class, Dad and I again found commonality in our love for radio dramas. Our local NPR station would play old serials, and our favorite was the classic

59

mystery-man saga *The Shadow*. A smile still creeps across my face and my eyebrows arch when I hear "who knows what evil lurks within the hearts of men?" Admittedly, I rarely hear this unless it's playing on my headphones, but still… goose bumps.

Scottie's musical tastes (and most kids', I'd wager) lean toward our own proclivities. She loves showtunes, and as mentioned is a big fan of Michael Jackson. A surprise, however, has been her love of classical musical. She discovered demo mode on our Roland Electric piano, something Colleen and I still can't figure out how to activate; I think it has something to do with sheer willpower, as this is all I've been able to glean from Scottie's technique. Upon demo activation, the piano cycles through about 5 or 6 classical pieces including Debussy's "Clair de Lune." Scottie equates this with ballet and immediately begins her own dance recital. A solemn moment, she expects Colleen and me to sit quietly and applaud after each piece. She reprimands an infraction of this rule. On rare occasions, she'll activate the demo and sit with me on the couch. Titling her head at me, she simply coos "Dada. I like dis." Me too, weewok. Me too.

The various *Guitar Hero* games, along with the recent *Alvin and the Chipmunks* movies, have given Scottie her primary introduction to classic rock. She insists on The Kinks' "You Really Got Me," because the Chipmunks open their *Squeakel* with the tune. *Guitar Hero* and its 99 sequels/spinoffs feature extensive playlists, and nearly every subsection of classic rock is represented. Save Metallica, who doesn't let anybody do anything with their music. Which is a shame, because I used to crank "Enter Sandman" through my flimsy plastic headphones all through junior high.

Time for an admission: I'm guilty of neglecting an essential piece of music geek tech. There's nothing like wrapping your ears in a good pair of headphones. What I own is nothing like a good pair of headphones. Sticking your head in a sublime set of cans and engaging your ears solely on the art of listening is a transcendent experience. Growing up, I used Pops' heavy-duty headphones he reserved only for his super-cool reel-to-reel system. Thankfully the system was equipped with a tape deck, so I could lie back on our fluffy tan carpet and tune out the world. Quite a few folks today listen to their tunes on their car radio, or through a small pair of external iphone speakers. As I write this I'm jamming to Dave Brubeck's *Time Out* album on my rinky-dink ipod ear buds. Though recently I've noticed a renewed interest in engaging the musical experience. Dr. Dre introduced his "Beats by Dre" line, high-end cans to satisfy your aural senses. Colleen borrowed a pair of her mom's noise-canceling headphones for our UK Trip, and I delight in using the still-to-be-returned pair.

Friends of mine who have children regulate music, particularly their P-Diddy, Lady Gaga, or whatever the hell it is you kids listen to nowadays. They fear that lyrics such as Gaga's "I want your ugly, I want your disease" will manifest themselves in their kids' speech. We don't worry about this all that much, since one of the harshest lyrics in our musical rep tends to be "now that we're dancing, who cares if we ever stop?" from *Hello Dolly!* Other G-rated titles include *Woody's Roundup*, a collection of country songs written and performed by Riders in the Sky, and one of her favorites, Daft Punk's lyricless score to *TRON: Legacy*.

No, our primary content challenges consist of movies and television programs.

***

Mimicry

My relationship with Dad was steeped in movie lore and metaphor. And rhyme, apparently. Anyhoo, from early childhood through early man-childhood, Dad and I duplicated many practices from the flicks. One of our favorites was "the Mookie" (from Spike Lee's *Do the Right Thing*). *Instructions: When greeting a fellow, rather than a handshake, pinch your thumb, index, and middle fingers. Shake as if sprinkling salt three times. That's the Mookie. Can be used as a congratulatory gesture in addition to a greeting. Dad instilled in me the mantra "do the right thing," a mantra echoed thematically (and in the title) by the Spike Lee Joint. It's an ideal I carry with me today, and one I

62

preach to Scottie. Though for the record, I won't show the film to her as early as Dad did to me. I was eleven.

Our other "thing" was a movie geek's expression of love. When particularly proud of one another, we'd of course hug, high five, and Mookie. On special occasions, or whenever the impulse drove us to it, we'd put our foreheads together and say "funny man, funny rain man". *Rain Man* (1988) and *Do the Right Thing* (1989) were released when I was 10 and 11 years old, and they were both rated R (completely justified ratings, in my opinion). This was the thing with Dad- he was perhaps a little too lenient with what films we'd see (*Predator* when I was 9), but I appreciated the trust and faith he placed in me.

I did end up breaking that trust after going to see *D.A.R.Y.L.* (Data Analyzing Robot Youth Lifeform) with my pal. I was seven, almost eight, and at the conclusion of our family-friendly film, we were supposed to wait for Dad to pick us up. I called him using an archaic device called a "pay phone" and told him we wanted to play arcade games for another couple hours. He said that was fine, but we were to wait outside when finished. Total deception, thanks to an alluring movie poster that commanded our attention. The decision was made: we would sneak into *Lifeforce*, an R-rated tale of naked space vampires who have to sleep with people. It was scary, and the lead vampire woman walked around completely nude the *entire film*. We didn't know what to think.

We came out of the film wide-eyed and full of giggles- and there was Dad. And I was in major trouble. Dad wasn't afraid I'd imitate the film. He was more upset that I'd lied. He even stated that if we'd asked, he might've been okay with us watching the movie, though I don't think he knew exactly what it was about.

Does this mean I'll allow Scottie to watch something like *Enter the Dragon*? Errr... as I've said, I fast forward to some of the tamer fight scenes, but I partially blame Colleen. She got me a shirt in Cambridge with cute versions of Bruce Lee and the *Enter the Dragon* cast. Scottie saw this and immediately recognized it. We then had to watch the opening fight scene- excuse me, opening "practice session." See? *Mainly* Colleen's fault for buying me a rad shirt. My point is, no, I won't let her watch those films now.

It's interesting to note that Colleen and I would watch some questionable material with her, most notably the *James Bond* films, before she was old enough to walk. She even got into all the Marvel films as she got older. But now, due to mimicry, we have to be incredibly careful. I'm sure most folks would say their children are imaginative. I hate to be brusque, but they're not. Not all of them.

Scottie is so imaginative, and her role play so deep, that every so often it's difficult to connect with her unless you enter the world with her. I'm not talking about our usual "Dada, I'm Jasmine and you be Aladdin", where we reenact a Disney film or even take the characters into new scenarios (the other day she was Snow White with Thor's hammer, Captain America's shield, and Hulk's hands, while I was Bottom from *A Midsummer Night's Dream*- the kid digs her Shakespeare). The difficulty occurred when she'd repeat a line or lengthy phrase, and even with a frame of reference there was no way to break her loop. She had to choose to come out of it on her own. She doesn't do this anymore, though the tendency to relate to things as if she's living in a film remains.

Another issue we encountered was with Disney's *Lilo and Stitch* of all things. As a film, it's one of my favorites Disney has produced. The relationships are incredibly clear yet complex, and nothing comes easily. Noni takes care of her younger sister Lilo, because both their parents recently died. They live in Hawaii, and while Lilo enjoys swimming and taking dance lessons, she has no friends. She's not particularly easy to get along with, and is prone to vocal outbursts and violence (she bites a cohort). Noni isn't the best parental figure, and has difficulty keeping a job. They both evolve and discover a sense of responsibility through the arrival of another outcast: the alien, Stitch. I love it, and so does Scottie.

After her first few viewings (probably on the same day), we noticed a shift in behavior. She'd scream in our faces "NOOOOO! I DON'T WANT YOU!" and even started biting us when faced with discipline, something she'd never even attempted prior to viewing the film. She hadn't started preschool, and interactions with other children never yielded this behavior. It came directly out of *Lilo and Stitch*. We switched it out of rotation (among *Aladdin*, *The Letter Factory* and *Nanny McPhee)* for a few months and after addressing the issue, she understood how unacceptable that behavior was.

Now, conversely, programs (primarily PBS) like *Super Why!* and *Curious George* have engaged her curiosity and bolstered her vocabulary. A favorite activity of mine is our running commentary, akin to *Mystery Science Theatre 3000*, as we watch George lose his waterproof camera to a sea lion. "Dat George!" she giggles. "He just lost it because he slides down da ice on his bottom." Me: "Yes. He received a chilly reception." Scottie: "Yeah, he's chilly. Cuz he's on da ice." We both throw our heads back and guffaw.

Super Why! boasts a favorite of mine- spelling. This is an area in which she's always excelled, and she's been able to point out our magnet letters on the fridge since she was a little over one. Positive mimicry evolved into comprehension as well as her own special vocabulary. She went so far as to change the lyrics on Super Why's song from "he's the guy, he's Super Why" to "dat's his plane, and he can fly".

I think most children engage in this form of mimicry. I vividly remember at the age of four (maybe it was five; not so vivid, I concede) getting up with Mr. Rogers when it was time to take a walk around the neighborhood. I'd circle Dad's oh-so-small living room in our teeny one bedroom apartment, telling him I'd be back at the end of the day.

As she's grown older, it's truly moving to see an increased awareness of her actions and their repercussions. She recently confessed with sadness and remorse: "I hit Claire on da hand wif a red broom at Music wif Miss Betty. I have to al- ap- apologize." Her teachers, and even Claire herself, were unaware of this incident but Scottie knew she'd done something unacceptable. After owning up, she sang along with the Sondheim tribute we had playing, and twirled with Anita during the *West Side Story* portion. As far as mimicry, she hasn't crossed the line into dangerous stunt territory- thus far she's been able to discern what Mum and Daddy disapprove of, and what will cause irreparable damage to her strong but fragile little body.

I failed to head my own instincts when, as a six year-old daredevil, I sprang from the top rung of our jungle gym's ladder. Pops had told me, rather nastily, that I wasn't at all like Superman. I set out to prove him wrong by an attempt at flight. I did a horrific belly flop and writhed around, the wind knocked out of me. Thankfully our red peeled-paint jungle gym wasn't more than six feet tall. Pops wasn't as sympathetic as I would've liked, as I recall.

Playing with proverbial fire (never really played with it literally), I again delved into the dark. As a kid, I didn't have any fear of spiders; on the contrary, they captivated me. I credit the Amazing Spider-Man. I actively sought out the arachnids, unconcerned with spider bites. Perhaps I secretly hoped one was irradiated and would imbue me with the ability to stick to walls and swing around the city. As an adult, I can't stand spiders. They're creepy-crawly, and they're awful, awful things.

We do encourage the use of our family slogan (complete with gestures) as it's uttered before every departure or sleep period. It's in three parts; first we make the ASL sign for 'I love you' while saying "I love you", then we invert it to look like Spider-Man's web shooting action and we proclaim "THWIP!" Next, both hands make the "loser" L, but with the thumb at 45 degrees instead of 90. In a gruff voice, we intone "good guys and gals!" The latter salutation comes from the John Carpenter epic *Big Trouble in Little China*. The good guys give the sign as if to say, "yep, we're awesome and we're good." Hence "good guys and gals". Once, Scottie and I played at the park and she realized "I'm da good gal, Dada, and you're da good guy!" That's it. She made the connection.

Another connection she became adept at was swearing in the exact tone as her Minga. This only manifested in her crib. We'd hear a loud "oh gaaddayyyymmmiiiittt!" and knew we had to rush into her room. This meant she'd reached her hand into a poop-filled diaper. Sure enough, there she'd be with crap on her hands and a disgusted look on her face. Sadly, she'd whisper "Mama Dada. Oh gadaymit."

There is a new thing I dislike: "you're going down; down, down, down!" It's never directed at anybody or anything, and is actually quite funny, but she won't tell me where she heard it. If anybody has a clue what this is from, please enlighten me.

Then there is our culture's fascination with guns. Like Batman, I've had a distaste for real-life firearms. Understand that fantasy guns were exempted from this. Remember, at the age of ten I carried an imaginary mini-gun, and blew away xenomorphs while reenacting scenes from *Aliens*. Around this time, Dad (certified anti-gun) got me a monthly membership to *Photon*, an athletic club of sorts, where grown folks and kids would run around zapping each other for points. Exactly like *Lazer Tag*, but way cooler. The environment was multi-story, and spectators above blasted at you with rail-mounted laser guns. It was epic. When not in the *Photon* arena, I'd find tree branches shaped like Drake's gigantic gun, or use wrapping paper tubes as lightsabers and rocket launchers. Fantasy weapons were wielded by almost all of my contemporaries in our grand battles.

I've handled and shot real guns many times- Pops was a hunter and he and my uncles would go hunting and use all the meat off anything they shot. But I never wanted to go with them, never wanted to kill something, to take another living thing's life. So I'd shoulder my BB gun or rifle and shoot cans in the woods, or line up various targets for practice. I loved it, and took pride in my marksmanship. I had no qualms about fishing, however. I loved fishing despite the moral dilemma of taking life. I justified it as a kid by deciding that hunting the deer never seemed essential; but on further evaluation, how essential was my recreational fishing? And damn if I don't love a good steak. Where would I draw the line? It's an issue I continually evaluate, especially when dealing with Scottie. As much as I'd like to shield her from, well, everything, I know it's a ludicrous wish.

Our learning comes from our experience. If we don't go out and experience life, how versed in the world can we possibly be? Phileas Fogg, the brilliant hero of Jules Verne's *Around the World in 80 Days*, knows everything and nothing about the world. He's spent his days amidst his library, gleaning all he can from the multitude of leather-bound volumes. Yet the man has never deviated from his path, never tasted life by venturing away from his hometown. Until that fateful day he lets his curiosity be swayed by a tempting wager to travel the world in eighty days.

I'm not about to permit Scottie to run scott free (punny?) around the world, nor will I shelter her till she's forty (a proposition that becomes more attractive every day, I'll admit). She's going to grow; she's going to learn in her own way, yet for gain and for loss, mass media has entered her vernacular. I'm confident, I think, that we can steer her

through the choppy waters of negative mimicry.

***

The Gems

I've largely left out the "givens"- the geek pantheon of

untouchable properties that will always be sacred to us and to our

children. I speak, of course, about the Muppets (and all of Jim Henson's

creations), the *Indiana Jones* trilogy, and the holiest of holies: the *Star

Wars* trilogy.

The Muppet Show has received constant play since Scottie was a

few months old, the first three seasons, anyway; perhaps when this sees

print we'll also have the fourth season available. Baby Scottie giggled

and gurgled (with purpose) whenever Kermit came onscreen to announce

"it's the Muppet Show, with our very special guest Gilda Radner!" Her

little limbs reached toward the screen for the frog, and she especially

enjoyed Miss Piggy's "Pigs in Space" segment. Our Muppet journey

came full circle when I took her to see the new Muppet movie written by

and starring Jason Segel, aptly titled *The Muppets*. Scottie broke into the

song "Am I Muppet or a Man" in the lobby, and by heaven, I joined her

despite the disapproving looks.

Sesame Street is another Henson classic that has lightened our

home and elicited numerous conversations with Scottie on the ways of the world since her birth (she spoke with her *eyes*). Currently, it's *Elmo's Potty Time* that notches higher than any other episode, although she certainly relishes any opportunity to visit the place where the air is sweet and friendly neighbors meet.

I'm most encouraged by the fact that the program recently celebrated its Fortieth Anniversary. Not only were Colleen and I reared on its sunny days, but children continue to learn from the same furry friends who taught me, and that sort of longevity and legacy warms my grizzled old heart. Granted Elmo's new, but the Count (a favorite of mine, modeled after a beloved Universal Monster) still has kids laughing while they count their Cheerios. Scottie chimes in, counting "One Mama! Ah, ah, ah! Two Mamas (pointing to me)- ah, ah, ah!" Thanks Count.

Other Henson works that entranced me as a kid haven't quite landed with Scottie. But I'm sure she'll start to dig *The Storyteller*, *Fraggle Rock*, and *The Secret Life of Toys* (as long as they're still on Netflix streaming). She does "dance magic dance" when *Labyrinth* plays, and she emulates the gelfling Jen's pipe playing in *The Dark Crystal*. Jim Henson's properties, particularly *Sesame Street*, have always reflected and blended pop culture well, and their parodies work for geeks both young and old. A shared favorite of Scottie's and mine is the epic "Texas Telly and the Golden Triangle of Destiny." The triangle-obsessed monster dons a fedora and uses his whip to assist him in his quest. For geeks and normies alike, this direct parody of another state-named fella should be fairly obvious.

Scottie's earliest exposure to the *Indiana Jones* trilogy occurred in the womb. Colleen was sitting on the couch watching *Last Crusade* while I put together Scottie's crib. Her room was still a work-in-progress, and this essential piece was needed before other projects could be tackled (per one of Colleen's famous lists). Though I'm no handyman, my hands flew across the rails, inspired by Indy as he and Elsa searched for the hidden Roman numeral Ten in the library. A twist of the Allen wrench and Indy and I simultaneously exclaimed "X marks the spot!" The crib was completed; Henry Jones, Jr. and I both prepared for the next phase of our respective journeys.

When a two-year-old Scottie begged to watch a movie, any movie, in an effort to again circumnavigate bedtime, Colleen and I looked at each other. "*Raiders of the Lost Ark?*" I gently asked, pleading with my eyes. Colleen smirked and agreed to it. Scottie wasn't particularly thrilled, but her desire to stay awake overrode her desire to have her way when it came to film choice.

A bit disinterested through the beginning (and we skipped past some of the scarier parts), I remember the exact spot she perked up. Indy grins as he picks up the idol, and with a cocky air begins to move away. A snap. The camera pushes in tight on Indy's shocked face. Then, the giant boulder barrels toward us, and at that instant Scottie bolted up in bed. With nary a noise, she stared at the screen, wondering how this gruff archaeologist could ever get out of this predicament. Colleen pulled Scottie's crazy curls out of her face, and I kissed the munchkin's head. Scottie brushed us both aside, and resumed her vigil until Indy leapt through the cobwebs and out of the cave, unharmed. She sighed, almost in a sweat, and flopped back against the pillows. She'd never been so quiet and I don't think she's ever been as silent since (she has quite the bellow).

The other Indy movies followed many more times save *Crystal Skull*. She, like her old man, has an affinity for Short Round. I always thrilled to the prospect of being Indy's sidekick. I realized I could never (at least at the age of six) be Indiana Jones himself but maybe, just maybe, I could learn enough Kung Fu to duke it out with Mola Ram's henchmen alongside Dr. Jones. Scottie emulates Shorty's kung fu punches and kicks on our bed, and I love it. Colleen loves and loathes it, simultaneously. This is a big reason DC Comics added Robin to Batman's side, as the connection with younger readers was essential to the company's bottom line.

To illustrate her growth from the time of *Lilo and Stitch* (she was a little over two) to now: a few nights ago, my three and a half year-old weewok and I were watching *Temple of Doom* (yes, I fast-forwarded past the heart-ripping-out scenes) and the part came up where Indy fights the Thuggee assassin in his room. The two have a slugfest, trading vicious blows until Indy envelops the hostile in his whip and tosses it into the ceiling fan, hanging the guy. Brutal and questionable material to be sure. Scottie asked questions and made comments throughout the entire thing, but the one that got me was her suggestion that "Indynana Jones should apologize to da guy for hitting." I explained that he was the bad guy and she considered this for a minute. "I know he's da bad guy, Dada, and dat Indynana Jones is da good guy. Dey need to say dere sorry for hitting." I can ask for no more.

George Lucas has been, in recent years, vilified for his mishandling of his franchises. I think some of it is justified, including the flak he's received for constantly re-cutting his films. But I look at Indy and Lucas' most successful franchise *Star Wars*, and I can't help but be grateful to the man for significantly shaping my youth. Growing older, I look at what he was able to accomplish with the original trilogy and I marvel. Hell, at the risk of losing geek cred, I marvel at what he's been able to sustain with the prequels and beyond. Before you scoff or toss this tome in Luke's funeral pyre beside Vader, please come along with me.

Star Wars permeates and subsists in our souls. You may have never seen the films (go watch the OT/Original Trilogy right now, please), but I guarantee someone close to you has a personal story about the saga across the stars. Cross-culturally, folks know the ways of the Force, Yoda's shuffle and scattered syntax, and Leia's metal bikini. For my friends and I, this geek foundation (I won't liken it to a virus) manifested in lightsaber fights with everything from the obvious flashlights to the less-obvious corn dogs. Seriously. A trip to Wienerschnitzel when I was nine ended in tears when my little brother Trampas and I whacked each other as hard as we could with our corn dogs. With Scottie, we fashion lightsabers out of paper towel tubes, and we also advocate invisible lightsaber battles in an effort to prolong the life of our IKEA furniture.

Scottie showed an interest in drumming early on, so I let her use my drumsticks for a spell (I'm not a drummer, but was put into *Blue Man Group*'s Drum School when the company was considering me for the show). She was very good about keeping the music on the practice pad. Until she wasn't. She decided to utilize the drumsticks as double lightsabers, and our 42-inch LED TV paid the price.

New generations of *Star Wars* fans continue to be cultivated, and not just because of their geeky parents. *Star Wars* toys consistently top sales, which is incredible for a long-dormant (now active) franchise. Fans have certainly kept the franchise alive through their demand of new product, and companies have risen to the occasion with new books, comics, and video games to satiate fans. Arguably the biggest reason for the resurgence, bigger even than the prequels, is the computer-animated series on Cartoon Network, *Star Wars: The Clone Wars*. As I write this, it's four seasons in and about to begin a fifth this fall. I haven't seen it, but I admit I'm intrigued. *Attack of the Clones* (*Episode II*) ends with the Clones flying off to war and *Revenge of the Sith* (*Episode III*) begins as the Clone Wars draw to a close. Ever since Obi-Wan Kenobi spoke of the "Clone Wars" in *A New Hope* (*Episode IV*), I'd dreamed of the epic conflict. Jedi versus Clones, and Luke's father was the most cunning warrior of all? Sign me up, both at the age of five and (based on that early description) now at the age of nearly thirty-five. Prior to *Episode III* and the current incarnation of the Clone Wars animated series, Cartoon Network presented a traditionally animated micro-series (2-3 minutes per episode) of the Clone Wars by Genndy Tartakovsky. Tartakovsky was responsible for the excellent animated series *Samurai Jack*, a show I'm going to watch with Scottie in the near future. All far more intriguing than the actual prequels.

At school, the kids (mostly boys and Scottie- see the chapter ***Princesses and Gender Roles***) know and love Star Wars. Scottie pretends to be Yoda, Princess Leia, Queen Amidala, or a wookie jedi, and the boys welcome her participation in their games of the Force. One of her little pals even has full-on Jedi powers, and force-pushes me when

I come to pick up Scottie.

Scottie has viewed all of the OT, but *Empire* was her first foray into the Star Wars mythos. She was all of one and a half, and I skipped over Hoth to the introduction of Yoda. She was slobbering down on some spaghetti in her lion booster chair, and her tiny jaw dropped when that little green Muppet popped up. "Away put your weapon! I mean you no harm!" Yoda, with a giggle in his voice and mystery to boot, locked eyes with Scottie and sucked her in. She pointed feverishly, spaghetti strands dangling off her index finger. "Scottie, that's Yoda," I informed her. "YOYA!" she yelled. "More Yoya!" More Yoya it was. Now that she's had a chance to view all the films (still no prequels) Yoda continues to be her most beloved Jedi pal.

Shopping for an infant before she arrives in your home is an interesting proposition for a man who's never really been around babies. I'd held a few babies, played with a ton of toddlers, but the ins and outs of the baby business eluded me. Granted, I never sought out the knowledge nor really had the need. I knew about pacifiers, knew their purpose. While shopping, Colleen grabbed a pack and said, "We need these binkies." Binkies? That sounded like "blankie", which is what I called my blanket. Makes sense. But 'binkie'? Where did they get that? Colleen informed me that she and her sister Renee referred to binkies as "bobos". "Can we compromise and call them Bobo Fetts?" I innocently asked. Colleen sighed, but went along with it. And so from day one until now, pacifiers are bobo fetts.

When she first began to speak, Scottie would reach for her pacifier proclaiming "Bobo Beyet!" I remember the first time watching *Jedi* with her, which was well after she'd mastered speech (perhaps 'mastered' is an exaggeration, but still). She pointed to various characters and asked "who's dat, Dada?" I answered even the obscure characters in Jabba's palace, but then she pointed to "da flying guy" and I told her that was Boba Fett. Her mind was blown. "Dat's like my bobo fett, but dat's his name," she surmised. Yes, my weewok. Now you know. And knowing is half the battle. G.I. Jooooooooooe!

With the advent of recording technology, when I was seven or eight I bought a blank VHS tape with my lawn mowing money so I could record the first *Star Wars* (before Dad bought me the official CBS Fox videocassettes from his movie-of-the-month club). Taping it straight off the TV and attempting to edit out commercials required ingenuity and guesswork. I became engrossed in the action and forgot to press record out of a commercial break. As such, the tape cut from the Millennium Falcon's approach on the Death Star to Han in the trash compactor shouting "One thing's for sure- we're all gonna be a lot thinner!" What media will be available to Scottie when she wants to make her own video mixtape? It'll be beamed directly into her brain by that point, I suppose.

The *Star Wars* saga, warts (prequels) and all, remains very dear to my geeky generation and me. If had to peg what geekdom is all about on one film series, *Star Wars* would be it. For better or worse- mostly for the better, I believe.

***

Media's Influence on the Parents

While certain fringe (and not-so fringe) groups would have us think that television and other media have single-handedly disintegrated our youth's minds and turned them into a bunch of hooligans, I obviously don't hold to this premise. I agree that you can't ignore the influential power of the media, but I've always believed this to be a gross oversimplification of a complex issue, and that the common sense of parental supervision should prevail. My play *Truth, Justice, and the Four-Color Way* was written about a little-known period in America's history in an effort to explore this very idea.

In the early to mid 50s, watchdog organizations put pressure on the government to blame juvenile delinquency on some tangible villain. Comic books were chosen, and televised Senate Subcommittee hearings began. Entertaining Comics was the hardest hit, and Publisher/Writer William M. Gaines was the scapegoat. Gaines' position was that parents needed to take responsibility for their offspring, and that kids don't mimic what they've seen in comics (not entirely true, Bill). As the playwright, I highly recommend reading/producing this play…

As illustrated earlier, Scottie engages in mimicry but has thus far been able to distinguish between reality and fiction. When watching Colleen and me on stage, she knows we're playing characters despite how deeply she's swept into the action. We're always aware of the need for media regulation. But what about regulating what *we* watch?

One of our "programs", *Parenthood*, strikes the obvious chords. How do you balance family with career, and a social life with equally important self-reflection? Thematically, we were hooked. Problems arise when the show (as well as the well-intentioned but over-informed internet) pushes us to think there are direct parallels to our family. Good drama should induce reflection, and find a commonality that binds us all together. Here's the issue with *Parenthood* as the media example. In the show, the lead's son is prone to outbursts, seems inattentive at times, and goes into his own imaginary world quite often. In the second or third episode, he's diagnosed with Asperger's syndrome.

Scottie had (and still has) the tendency to create lush worlds in her imagination, and it was quite difficult to pull her out. During her third birthday at preschool she threw a tantrum, and was incredibly shy and withdrawn. Her teachers and we attributed it to the melding of two disparate worlds, something Colleen and I both had/have issues with reconciling. Scottie has gotten better about us entering her school world, but you can tell she likes to keep family and school separate. Colleen and I worried- does she have a problem for which we should be seeking help? It's interesting to note that a dear family member has been diagnosed with Asperger's but we hadn't ever really scrutinized Scottie's behavior exhaustively until we saw a trigger on television. Her growth has thankfully alleviated many fears, but every time we sit down to watch that guy from *Sports Night* and that gal from *Con Air* go through the tribulations of *Parenthood*, we definitely reconsider our own trials.

Another source for my neuroses is perhaps the most difficult to police: the Internet. The advent of viral videos, and Facebook 'likes' and 'shares', makes the transmittal of media instantaneous and wide reaching. It's also alarmingly unregulated. Some famous viral videos (internet memes) from the early days of the Internet made my playlist, including the Trololololo guy, the Winnebago Man, and the wild *Star Wars* kid (over 25 million views on YouTube). The latter features a portly 15-year-old flinging around a golf club like a lightsaber. As a fellow geek, I ask you- who hasn't done something similar? I used corn dogs, for crying out loud. The kid filmed himself, and some fellow students snagged the tape, digitized it, and uploaded it to the Internet. Enterprising rotoscopers even added lightsaber effects and John Williams' music (which is actually quite cool). The kid was humiliated, and ridiculed by his classmates. His parents filed a lawsuit in 2003, citing the public embarrassment as a reason their son dropped out of high school and checked into a child's psychiatric ward at a Canadian hospital. And we're all guilty of fueling this type of harassment; nowhere is it more prevalent than from behind the computer screen.

There's a distance we enjoy, and even posting with your name still presents a level of anonymity. The Internet allows for completely free expression, and that freedom occasionally translates into a freedom from common courtesy and respect. Scottie herself could one day go viral, but how to protect her? I'd go berserk if I discovered she was being picked on at school, but what happens when she's ridiculed by millions of Internet bullies? What are the consequences? Not to mention the web content she could access, even with content locks. Scary stuff for a parent.

After a game at our local racquetball club, Dad would regularly leave me to hit the ball around by myself while he sat in the sauna and showered off. I'd wander around sometimes and get to know the employees. Around the age of six or seven I discovered some of the guys hanging out in the supply closet. They knew me, knew Dad, and invited me to come in. Various centerfolds from Playboy were tacked up on the walls, and a collection of Playboys was completely visible on the magazine rack. As the weeks went on, they'd invite me in every so often to hang out, play cards, and talk about racquetball. Dad came looking for me one day and saw me sitting in there with all these pictures of naked women, Playboys at my feet.

Now, Dad loved the ladies and he was no prude (remember all the R-rated movies we watched?), but he was not about to let this stand. He read 'em the riot act, and that was that. I wasn't allowed to wander off from the racquetball court unless he went with me. What would he have done had the Internet existed?

***

The evolution of media

Though radio has declined in the past ten years, it's been a remarkably slow decline. I'd wager most people don't even own a traditional radio anymore; most likely some sort of dock for the iphone that also happens to serve as a clock radio. I find that most of my listening to traditional radio occurs in the car. Folks love their morning shows, and despite the prevalence of digital music players, a good old in-dash stereo still comes standard on the majority of automobiles. But radio stations have evolved to develop an online presence, as well as the ability to be played on mp3 devices.

Sirius XM Radio is another natural evolution of the medium. It allows on-demand listening, custom stations, and sports radio out the wazoo. I've thought about purchasing it, though I've never taken the plunge, in the event I find myself on a long-distance drive during a

Bengals game. Talk radio continues to entice listeners as much as it did when I was growing up with Howard Stern and the like. And despite massive budget cuts, NPR thrives both online and over standard radio waves through listener loyalty and support.

When I received my first ipod, a video click-wheel version, I fell in love with podcasts. Free downloads of interviews with screenwriters (Jeff Goldsmith's *The Q&A* receives steady play), analysis shows on football and comic books (independent of one another), and even re-broadcasts of old-time radio serials can be found after a simple search. Any niche (geeky) interest appears to be represented, and I'm amazed at the quality of self-recorded podcasts. We used to do our own version of this as kids: I'd bust out the gigantic tape recorder and conduct interviews with my friends on subjects like street magic and cafeteria food. This was my earliest venture into writing, as I began scripting comedy skits and recording all the parts myself. Childhood shenanigans, but had the internet existed I would surely have published it online.

Dad's childhood in Great Depression-era NYC presented him with a dilapidated radio as his main (and mostly affordable) means of entertainment. Sure he played stickball and stoopball in the streets, but my Grandma would summon him in before dinner to listen to the Yiddish radio program "Ho Americanskimo!" and the peppy tones of Guy Mitchell's "feet up, pat him on the po-po." When his parents weren't around, Dad would sneak-listen to radio serials, and one of his favorites was *The Shadow*.

It should come as no shock that he brought me up with the radio equally alongside movies, television, literature, and sports. When *The Shadow* episodes were available on cassette tape, Dad bought the whole collection. On nights when he'd have custody of me for sleepovers, we'd listen to Lamont Cranston's scary voice intimidating criminals: "Who knows what evil lurks in the hearts of men? The Shadow knows... BWAHAHAHAHAHAHAHAHAHA!"

Between the ages of five and ten, I especially liked listening to Larry King. Well, I didn't have a choice since Dad insisted the dial stay tuned to Larry's show. He always interviewed somebody interesting, but I remember planning a call-in question when he announced Stan Lee as next week's guest. I was probably seven, and drooled (perhaps literally) at the prospect of asking Stan the Man a question about my beloved Marvel Superheroes. I forget what I asked him. And nearly twenty years later when I actually met the man he couldn't remember either. But it was a cool conversation, nonetheless. What did we talk about the second time? Big Little Books, as it turns out. Specifically, that Incredible Hulk Big Little book Dad gave me when I was three- the book that more or less taught me to read.

When the radio wasn't enough, my compadres and I would make

our own mixtapes, recording various songs off the radio for one ultimate megamix. I wish I could replicate the mixtape a coworker gave me for my end-of-college sojourn from New Mexico to the wilds of California. It was such a pivotal time for me, and every song makes me recall a different stop or stretch of Interstate 40. 21 years old, and freshly graduated from college, I packed up everything I owned and set out for the West Coast. My pal from the Warner Brothers Studio Store slipped me a clear purple cassette tape before I left. "And be sure to visit Golden Apple Comics when you get to LA," was his parting advice. With the truck loaded, and my dark blue Ford Ranger towed behind, I slipped the tape into the deck and set off on my epic journey. The genius of this particular mixtape was the choppy sound bites interspersed between songs. The whole tape started off with Mako's opening speech in *Conan the Barbarian*: "Let me tell you of the days of high adventure!" VWOOOOOOOM, DUM, DUM, DUM DUM kicked in and the Beastie Boys' *Sabotage* blasted through the Ryder truck's tinny and (tiny) speakers. Solid sounds like Stereo MCs' *Connected*, Sublime's *Doin' Time*, and *Little Brown Bag* off Tarantino's brilliant *Reservoir Dogs* soundtrack kept me truckin' down the road. The tape ended with the scene between Luke and Vader in *Empire*- the entire scene, concluding with Luke's weenie "Nooooooooooooooo!" yell. I loved it.

That tape marked a time in '99 when geeks endured a level of anticipation not encountered previously during my lifetime. We were *Star Wars* fans and had little idea how badly *Episode I* one would suck. I was a senior at the University of New Mexico. *The Phantom Menace* loomed, and we frothed at the mouth at every nugget released. We attended the midnight release of the toys at Toys R' Us. 21- and 22-year-old men having lightsaber fights in the toy store's aisles. That's where I bought my Darth Maul inflatable chair, which I'd later use to wait in line overnight for tickets to the film. Not for the film itself- that was a line weeks later- just for the tickets. The *amuse-bouche* was the trailer itself. My roommate, Steve, owned the only computer in the house capable of handling the download. To download a trailer today (full screen and high-definition) could take as little as ten seconds, depending on the connection speed. Back in 1999, Steve's super-duper computer downloaded a miniscule version of the *Episode 1* teaser trailer (about the size of a pack of chewing gum) in a measly **five hours**. Ah, what a stellar time to be a geek- full of hope and child-like wonder. Hearing any song off that mixtape now immediately thrusts me back there.

Mixtapes of the present are smoothly mixed into digital playlists through GarageBand or ProTools, and downloading a trailer or song to your smartphone or tablet takes seconds. Back in the day, I literally spent years searching for a particular CD or cassette. I had to go to the Virgin Megastore in Vegas to find my sweet Nordic soul groove, "She Gave Me

Love", from The Getaway People's self-titled debut.

Besides my 80s tunes, I was a jazz geek growing up with Dad's sensibilities. He dug Nat King Cole, Basie and Ellington, and the dulcet sounds of Cool Jazz. My jazz horizons were broadened when I took a Jazz History course in college, and I traveled all the way down the rabbit hole. Our professor played a tune on the piano that was the opening riff of Nat Adderly's "The Work Song." I dug it and asked how to find a recording. The best my professor could muster was a "good luck" shrug. I discovered it was on Cannonball Adderly's live album *Nippon Soul*, and I had to have it. Tracking it down took over a year. Yes, I had email. But it was finally a tangible letter (on paper!) I sent to a jazz enthusiast in Europe that yielded me a copy of this masterpiece. I recently typed the album into Google, and a page and a half of purchasing options appeared. Oy. The sax definitely sounds better if I worked to find it, dammit.

I've spoken a bit about the Netflix streaming service, and I still marvel at the ease with which we acquire our digital content. I'm talking about legal methods, none of this torrent stuff (though that's another book's worth of opinions). And it's as simple as plug and play with the Apple TV and Roku boxes, each of which is the size of a small candy box. Any show we desire pops up quickly, and I could spend a virtual lifetime watching the films and television shows on my Netflix instant queue alone. I'm tempted to make a nonsensical purchase and subscribe to the recently launched Warner Archive streaming channel. The Roku-exclusive channel enables the instant stream of titles from the Warner Brothers library, many of which have been out of print (or never even seen print). The pulp classic *Doc Savage* remains one of the most tantalizing titles. But I will abstain… for now. With Hulu and Netflix each at 8 bucks a month, Amazon streaming at 80 bucks for the year, and now Warner Archive for less than 10 a month (not to mention PBS.org for *Downton Abbey* and *Sherlock* episodes), more folks are cutting the cable cord and moving online.

Along with the ease of downloading comes the ease of interface. Scottie and her younger cousin AJ adeptly flip through shows and clips on iphones and ipads, and Scottie can actively surf the Internet to find the Michael Jackson video she desires. And this freaks me out a bit. In my day (oh dear), you had to work to find corruption. About as scandalous as we'd get was throwing the Sports Illustrated Swimsuit Issue into our library books and snickering during Geography class.

Even with parental locks, I worry less about Scottie's website choices than about who can contact her, take advantage of her, and get her locked up in a Nigerian scam to reclaim her lost millions (I daren't go any more severe for my own fragile psyche). We're starting to set boundaries for her, and limit her electronic consumption (something we've tried many times). Ultimately, I trust that we'll raise her with an appropriate balance when it comes to media. I trust...

***

The last (but certainly not final) word on cinema

Dad was instrumental in procuring my first legitimate job at 16 (I'd previously mowed lawns and worked in an apprenticeship at a landscaping company- no work permit, and I was paid under-the-table). His "special lady friend's" daughter worked at a second-run movie theatre, and they were hiring projectionists. It was a non-union position (most projectionists in Albuquerque belonged to the local 24601 or something) and I loved working with film. We had to build movies, reel by reel. You spliced the heads and tails together, and I stand by the fact that cinema splicing is an art unto itself. It can be done badly and ruin the film (when I saw a midnight showing of *Indiana Jones and the Kingdom of the Crystal Skull* the film was poorly spliced so it started out of frame, skipped at reel changes, and the bulb burned the film due to loose splices). For the *Empire Strikes Back* re-release in 1997, the film was mis-spliced and when Obi-Wan warns, "that boy is our last hope", Yoda's crucial response "no, there is another" was cut! Utter blasphemy. And sho nuff, I complained to management. In the short time between writing this and the time you've gotten it into your hands, I wouldn't be surprised if even more movie theatres switch to completely digital projection, avoiding issues like those described above. Of course none of that crap happened on **my** watch. There were other shenanigans in the projection booth (drinking, dancing, and debauchery), but none concerning the film's presentation.

During my high school tenure at the movie theatre (I continued working at various movie theatres well into college), I was privy to many pivotal films of the early-mid 90s. Dad shared the majority of these with me, and I think our last film together before he died was *Batman Forever* (you can't win 'em all). *Aladdin, The Nightmare Before Christmas, Jurassic Park*, Baz Luhrmann's *Strictly Ballroom, Tombstone,* Guillermo del Toro's *Cronos*, Robert Rodriguez's *El Mariachi, Batman: Mask of the Phantasm, Pulp Fiction, Clerks*, and even *Showgirls* are the ones that stick out on the movie screen of my mind.

In college, I spent my work-study as the Projection Manager at the University's Southwest Film Center. More splicing and more awesome films: Peter Jackson's *Heavenly Creatures*, Danny Boyle's *Shallow Grave*, Jet Li's *Bodyguard from Beijing*, anime classic *Ghost in the Shell*, and cult midnight movies like *Evil Dead* and Jackie Chan's *Drunken Master*. I ate, drank, and slept movies.

Growing up, Mom had custody of me until the end of my fifth grade year. Dad would get me for brief durations during the year, but summer was our big hangout time. For one month, we spent every day together. As soon as Mom dropped me off, Dad would get me some Squirt and we'd sit down to make THE LIST. Every place I wanted to visit, every movie I wanted to see. Eddie Murphy in *The Golden Child*? Done. A movie based on our favorite radio serial, *The Shadow*? Let's do it. For every movie viewed Dad made me write a review. I balked at this, but he threatened never to go to the cinema again. He also offered me a quarter per review. Sold. I wrote about *Ernest Goes to Camp* ("any age would like it, but the scene of playing poker and drinking beer isn't suitable for the very young folk"), *Creepshow 2* ("it doesn't even deserve meals"), and *Project X* ("a weird science-fiction movie, really made a monkey out of me").

That's not to say we didn't see flicks when I was with Mom and Pops. Mom took me to see Tim Burton's *Batman* in the summer of '89, just before my twelfth birthday. The door to the theatre swung open while we waited, and I peeked in to catch a glimpse of Vicki Vale cryptically whispering, "I know". Know what? What did she mean? Alfred drove away, the camera tilted up and Danny Elfman's music swelled. I pulled back from the door, not wanting to spoil the end (or any of it). Mom smiled and squeezed my hand. We were going to see a Batman movie, and I couldn't believe it. That same summer, Dad taped the 1966 Batman TV show marathon, culminating in *Batman The Movie* starring the purrrfect Lee Meriwether. I thrived in the world's resurrected

93

Batmania.

A note on Burton's *Batman*- you may think because it broke through into the collective mainstream consciousness that it was actually cool to like Batman. Yes and no. I was still ostracized by the "cool" kids (though my friends and I geeked out at the truly <u>Dark</u> Knight). And I was ostracized by Pops for wanting to see *Batman Returns* during a family vacation to Colorado. Pops' argument was that "Vacation's not for seeing movies." That was the most ludicrous statement I'd ever heard. And he lost.

One of the biggest thrills of my life centers around the local Cineplex. Dad took me to *Timerider* (though it wasn't entirely appropriate) and it was the first time I'd seen a film of his on the big screen. Happily munching on a Rax roast beef sandwich (better than Arby's, in my opinion), I watched as Dad (as a Mexican villager) screamed, "el Diablo has come!" Fred Ward's motorcycle rider from the future blew through town in a red suit, and Dad whipped the villagers into a frenzy. Pride (and roast beef) filled me. It was the perfect synthesis of our love of movies, and growing up as the son of an actor.

With Dad, the "appropriateness" of a film came into play on very few occasions. I do this differently with Scottie, or at least I attempt it. *Captain America* (the new one, not the 90s version with JD Salinger's son and the Italian sometimes-Red Skull) contains a scene where Cap chucks a guy off a plane and he disintegrates in the propeller. Seeing it, even though it occurs quickly, is somehow more acceptable to me than Pat Roach going through the plane's propeller in *Raiders* like a radish through a Cuisinart. I'd be more apt to let Scottie see any of the Marvel movies than *The Dark Knight* (which I wouldn't let her watch for quite a few years) or even the more benign (which isn't much) *Batman Begins*. It's always guns that get me. Even Bats beating the shit out of a thug is more acceptable to me (for her) than Arnie plugging dudes with a minigun, even if he is given the "don't kill anyone" directive from Eddie Furlong.

Terminator 2 was another R-rated film that we flocked to in droves. I remember my flannel bought at the 50 off store covering up my neon blue T2 shirt: the rad shirt had a T-800 skull and the phrase "I told you I'd be back." A cheesy shirt, and a total knockoff, but perfectly appropriate for the first showing. I'll always remember that flannel/shirt combo every time I view or discuss *T2*.

Many things trigger recollections of stories, but with most movies I can usually remember the specific time of my life. I may equate the film with a general feeling, or an event minutely related. I went to go see *The Relic* in Colorado with Ron, and left the theatre in my recently acquired Ford Ranger. The tiny pickup truck zigzagged (unintentionally) in the Denver snow. That one film (which was mostly forgettable) triggers memories of an entire trip that isn't part of a regular recollection.

Stories might be the most important element in our family unit, and I would argue for all humanity (I'll discuss this in the *Living the Example* chapter). All of these films and television shows I've mentioned tell stories worth our time and focus. Storytelling teleports us instantly, and that ability is extraordinary. A master filmmaker is a master storyteller.

Scottie, Colleen, and I went to see Martin Scorcese's *Hugo* in 3D, a celebration of the origins of cinema and the need to acknowledge and preserve it as an art. Scottie fell head first into the story of an orphan living in a train station who attempts to unlock his deceased father's secrets. But with that understanding comes a connection to his father and a way to bridge the vast ocean of death that has separated them. While Colleen and I appreciated and loved the film, Scottie followed every bit of it with intrigue. She quietly made comments, and once it was over continued them at full volume: "Dat movie was great! Da little boy lost his Daddy but he had da little girl to help him." She also made note of Sacha Baron Cohen's bad guy stationmaster: "He's fwawed (flawed). He just needed someone to love him and den he's nice now. Dey all like da magic guy's movies. I like da movies too." Tears from Colleen and me enabled another tender response from Scottie. "Why you crying? Mama, Dada- it's okay. Da little boy is okay. Let's go get M&Ms." The power of a well-told story. And of concession snacks.

5: The Printed Page

The. End. Two of the first words Scottie learned to read. Every board book (made up of four or five heavy cardstock pages), every children's book we read to her, even if we left off in the middle of a chapter, would conclude with us (all of us) saying "the end."

One of the cooler board books we received was a vinyl-coated volume by Sandra Boynton: *Bath Time!* "Hey! Hey! What do you say? It's time to take a bath today!" the opening page invites. Its binding makes it perfect for bath time, and Scottie has loved the adventures of its Pig hero since she was a baby. She couldn't wait to flip through to the back cover where "The End" was scrawled on a towel covering the lead character's piggy butt. The double entendre was never lost on her, though recently she especially giggles with glee when we reach this point.

Books featured prominently into our parenting plan literally from day one. In my delirium, I think I read Scottie the hospital menu hours after she was wheeled into the room to rejoin Mama. We resolved that no book-based movie would be viewed without going through the source material first, though we have wavered slightly on this point.

Dad was an English teacher, and a huge advocate of his children reading as soon as possible. As added incentive (beyond the titles themselves) he bribed/rewarded me with goodies: Charleston Chews, trips to the zoo, and monster walks (where I'd stand on his feet, and we'd walk around together like Frankenstein's monster).

Due to his profession, Dad packed our house to the gills with literature. The shelves were filled with Woody Allen comedy books, the philosophy of Kahlil Gibran, and the MLA Handbook (you may ask yourself "why doesn't he adhere to its rules in the body of this book?" Answer: rebellion and clarity). Like the toy Bookworm I owned, you never saw me without a copy of something or other in my hand.

Mom was also a teacher and massive volumes of encyclopedias were stacked around the living room. I devoured these. For the younger folks in the crowd, encyclopedias are massive books containing all the accumulated knowledge of the human race. You could use them as stepping stones across the Atlantic and only get through the letter M, as each volume might be Aa through Al, and so on. Encyclopedias were my Internet. One entire volume of our science encyclopedias (a fun thirty volume subset) dealt entirely with science experiments you could do without parental supervision (granted we ignored the "parental supervision *recommended*" stamp on the inside front cover). My younger brothers and I built a crystal radio, a foaming volcano, and even a device that created clouds. I kid you not- these books could have out Macgyvered Macgyver.

While reading these delightfully heavy encyclopedias, one topic would cause me to look up another topic. It's like the Internet now- I'll be researching a subject and something will be mentioned that makes me Google another topic. Exploring all these threads was as gratifying then as it is now. Following all these branches created more questions, and the search for answers. As a sophomore, a sign greeted you over the door when entering my biology teacher's classroom. "HAVE YOU EXTENDED YOUR DENDRITES TODAY?" Dendrites, our teacher explained, are tiny threadlike branches in your brain, and when you make a connection or learn something new these synapses fire and connect. I thought I could feel my dendrites extending every time I got to the end of an encyclopedia entry and it said **"cross reference with FUNGI."** Gleefully, I journeyed to the bookshelf for the appropriate volume. Dendrites extended, baby.

***

See you in the funny papers

Dad taught Greek mythology in his junior high English classes, and one of his teaching tools was the use of a series called *Classics Illustrated.* Exactly what it sounds like, each issue would abridge classic works of literature and present them in comic book form. The first comic I ever read was one of Dad's *Classics* featuring Homer's epic poem, *The Iliad.* I swallowed it whole, and wanted more of both comics and mythology. I took immediate ownership- these adventures became *my* adventures. I was on the road with Theseus as he warded off bandits and defeated the Minotaur barehanded, and I soared with Icarus dangerously close to the sun. *My* wings held together, however. Just barely.

Edith Hamilton's *Mythology* was a daily habit for me, and I owned the complete texts of *The Iliad*, *The Odyssey*, and *The Aeneid*. Very few of these myths had seen celluloid in the way I'd envisioned them (the disappointment would continue), however it was incredibly cool to watch Jason battle Ray Harryhausen's skeletons in the film version of *Jason and the Argonauts*. And *Clash of the Titans*, for all its cheese, provided glorious mythology for my four-year-old eyes. Perseus slugging it out with the Kraken while Zeus (Laurence freaking Olivier!) looked down from Olympus... it was mythology crack, and I couldn't get enough. So I read even more, expanding to Roman and Norse mythology.

The revelation that Stan Lee transplanted Thor from the thunder god's Norse mythology roots smack into the Marvel Universe rocked my world. Not only was Stan the Man using characters from Norse lore, but he also thrust Thor and his compatriots straight into the New York City of Spider-Man and the Avengers. And Thor's dialogue was almost Shakespearean in meter and tone. "Verily, foul demon, I shall smite thee so handily that the Frost Giants of Jotunheim shall not recognize thy visage!" was a common expression of rage from the Thunder God.

I was always aware of superheroes through many different media, and one of my earliest solo reading adventures at the age of three was that *Big Little* book I mentioned featuring the Hulk. I quickly launched more reading exploits, including a mail-away Spider-Man comic you could get through saving ALL laundry detergent tabs. I actually got into the collecting aspect of fandom rather late in the game. At our racquetball club, Dad used his "connections" to track down a comic that was noteworthy enough to make it into *Time* magazine. I became a collector when Dad triumphantly presented me with the first issue of the mainstream/geek crossover event of the day- the death of Robin four-issue storyline, titled *Batman: A Death in the Family*. I was eleven and this was released months before the mania created by Tim Burton's first *Batman* movie, so even though normal folks were aware of it, it was still geeky. Of course, I didn't care a bit.

For the remaining three issues, Dad made the mistake of taking me to our local comic book retailer, Comic Warehouse, and that was all the exposure I needed. An entire store devoted to Daredevil's exploits in Hell's Kitchen, Flash's trials and travails in Central City, and even local comic book creators' new characters duking it out in the Duke City (that's, uh, Albuquerque). Wide-eyed, and with my jaw almost literally on the floor, I strolled through the racks, picking up and flipping through nearly every comic. The majority of my money from then on would go toward collecting twenty copies of *Silver Surfer #50* (with its silver embossed cover), and every alternate cover of Jim Lee's re-launched *X-Men #1*.

Comics in the early 90s provided the largest sales in the industry's history. To capitalize on the craze, *Wizard Comic Magazine* was launched in 1992, with Todd McFarlane's *Spawn* on the cover. Since comic book movies were few and far between, fans could only dream of their heroes given proper justice on the big screen. One of my favorite features in *Wizard* was their monthly "Casting Call" section. They'd take a comic and cast their dream movie. The tone of the column was sardonic- there was no way anybody would ever make a *Spider-Man* movie, right? Surely *Iron Man*, let alone *The Avengers*, would never see the light of a projector. When their dream cast for the *X-Men* movie included genre fave Michael Biehn as Cyclops and hirsute rocker Glen Danzig as Wolverine, fandom rejoiced. But sadness crept in, because again we realized we'd probably never seen any of these in our lifetimes.

In later years, other geek events captured the media's attention, though not until the first *X-Men* film stormed into theatres in 2000 was geekdom made truly mainstream. Since killing Robin had worked so well (though in true comic book fashion he returned, despite editor Denny O'Neil's quote that "it would be a really sleazy stunt to bring him back"), DC orchestrated other catastrophic events including the death of Superman (he came back with a mullet) and the breaking of Batman's back by Bane (5Bs!).

Comics were a natural extension to the mythology I was reading concurrently; indeed, they're considered to be a modern mythology for this generation and the next. I was convinced as a child that my ideal job would be as a comic artist. That desire was squashed quickly when I attempted to draw Bart Simpson and he looked like Mother Theresa. My dream shifted to one day owning a comic book shop- that seemed much more feasible (and is still on my list). In fact, my favorite job that wasn't acting or writing (and it beat a few acting/writing gigs) was as a comic shop employee at the House of Secrets (it's on Olive in Burbank, close to Disney Studios- tell Paul and Erik that Lance sent you and they'll give you a noogie or something). It was at the House of Secrets that I met Adam and through him, his producing partner Jenette Kahn. Jenette (the former head of DC Comics!), called me and asked if I'd consider working for their production company whose emphasis was comics. I didn't think about it too long.

Trading comics raged through middle school, though I wasn't as keen on the trading aspect as much as I was the "I'll lend it to you and please return it to me in a week because I want to read it now that I pulled it from my longbox". I knew every single comic book in my collection and before I sadly whittled it down (I had to sell a large part of it to help pay for a film I produced, among other things) I was up to 12 longboxes with 300 comics in each. Math geeks? Yep, 3600 comic books. I remember where I got each one, and the circumstances surrounding each of them. I could recount each comic's contents, including creative teams and, in some cases, the ads. The inside front and back covers were usually reserved for video games. You had a badass shot of Solid Snake for the original *Metal Gear* on the inside front, while plastered on the back inside was Fabio's mug for *Ironsword: Wizards and Warriors II* (in the early 90s the man was not just on the covers of Mom's romance novels, but cereal boxes and other bizarre products).

Comics provided values, vocabulary, and virtue to me. Stan Lee and Steve Ditko appropriated one of the greatest things ever written (by Voltaire, whose *Candide* is still on my "to read" list) for their original *Spider-Man* comic. Uncle Ben, Peter Parker's stoic guardian, imparts this crucial and historic piece of wisdom:

"With great power there must also come-- great responsibility."

This, in its shortened form "with great power comes great responsibility", was my mantra from the age of four through, well, the present. Now, I believe we all are capable of and possess great power, therefore we all have a great responsibility to our community and to our fellow human beings. This was reinforced in several of Spidey's comics. Cops, firefighters, and the citizens of New York banded together to do what was right, aiding the superheroes that worked alongside them, not above them.

Some of the best moments of the Sam Raimi Spidey films encompass this spirit. In the first one, NYC residents throw sticks and stones (literally) at the Green Goblin while Spidey rescues passengers on a tramway. In part two, Spidey nearly sacrifices himself to save a runaway El train. He collapses onto the floor, and when Doc Ock shows up the passengers band together to protect the hero.

Dad always liked to impart lessons, and I responded well to a sermon (much to my own amazement). During an issue of Marvel's *What If?* Captain America decks a bad guy and, standing over his vanquished foe, remarks "it's at times like these that I recall the words of Lord Acton: 'power corrupts and absolute power corrupts absolutely.'" Who was Lord Acton? I looked him up in one of our gigantic encyclopedias. Extending those dendrites, any words in the pages of my comics like 'degradation' or 'infinitesimal' demanded repeated visits to the dictionary.

It thrilled me when comics would reflect heroes from other literature. Even as a kid it seemed obvious to me that Bob Kane and Bill Finger were influenced by Sherlock Holmes and Zorro when shaping the character of Bruce Wayne/Batman (incidentally, Bruce's parents were killed after a viewing of Douglas Fairbanks' *The Mark of Zorro*).

While Scottie was aware of superheroes early on thanks to the Marvel movies and TV shows, I didn't start actively reading comics to her until around her second birthday. An issue of Iron Man had been left out and Scottie ambled over to it. "Dis Iron Man," she discovered herself. It was as if she was amazed he could exist onscreen (yes, she'd seen the first *Iron Man* film as a two year old) and still find time to make an appearance in the colorful pages of a comic book.

The first comic that she herself picked out was a Batman/Young Justice book on Free Comic Book day. Once a year, usually the first weekend in May, comic retailers purchase specially packaged comics from publishers and give them out to customers for free. This frequently coincides with a big comic book movie (this year it's Marvel Studios' *The Avengers*), drumming up even more interest and business in the funny papers (as Pops calls them). I also grabbed a Walt Disney comic for her, but she was far more engrossed in reading about Robin and his superhero team Young Justice than checking out the shenanigans of Uncle Scrooge and his nephews. If I recall correctly, that was the weekend the mighty *Thor* made his big screen debut.

Her interest in comics ebbs and flows, though whenever I present a new comic to her she flings her arms up, solicits a flight around the room, then inquires "we read it?" Both Marvel and DC publish titles geared toward kids, and I applaud the other great titles for sale by independent publishers and the shops that promote youth titles. Unfortunately most comic book shops fit the stereotype- dingy, creepy places where the retailer evokes the Comic Book Guy on *The Simpsons*. This is truly a shame, as retailers should endeavor to change this stereotype; many have, including the aforementioned House of Secrets. Like theatre (see the next chapter), it's important to cultivate and enrich the next generation of patrons. A shop that displays Adult-only books in plain view, and employs clerks who feel the need to swear every other word while discussing why Superman could beat Hulk in a brawl, is destined to have an insular and uninviting client base. You want to market your shop to adults? Fine. Seriously. I'm no prude. But don't stock *Adventures in Reading starring the Amazing Spider-Man* (Spidey versus the Troglodyte, who's bent on using a bazooka to zap himself into famous literary works- no lie) and expect only thirty-year-olds to take a gander.

***

Stories

Comic shops continue to thrive, but the advent of online outlets has caused traditional brick and mortar lit havens to dry up. Thankfully the wonderful Adams Avenue Bookstore around the corner from our place has given all three members of our household spectacular flights of fancy. I dig books- in this age of Kindles, Nooks, and ibookstores it's easy to get caught up in the convenience of carrying around thousands of books on a device no bigger than a thin paperback. And I love my Kindle. It's incredibly convenient and the e-ink makes for a pleasant reading experience. But the tangibility of thumbing through a yellowed copy of, say, Ray Bradbury's *Dandelion Wine*, appeals to my sense of the present. We won't be around forever and neither will the book I hold in my hand. Though it shows its age, you can't help but feel that this book unlocked amazing worlds for a previous reader and if you're patient enough to crack the cover, you too can discover El Dorado.

While I actively sought out novels, Dad also supervised my book path, introducing manuscripts that were maybe a few years beyond me. Nevertheless, it's been fun to revisit books I read as a kid. *The Catcher in the Rye* was a particular favorite of mine. Like Holden Caulfield, I unfortunately reveled in being a wise-ass. As a balding man (you'll notice from my author photo that I've forsaken a few follicles myself), Dad decided to partake in the hair-sweeping craze of... never. Why did guys do this? Inevitably, Dad would get caught up in a blustery day, and there went his mane. I gave him so much grief, going so far as to call him a phony since Holden called all hair sweepers "phonies." Poor Dad stopped sweeping from that day on. I did it in such a way as to be rude; not funny or ironic. Dad didn't speak to my lack of manners, and it's something I feel terribly about. I claimed it was his fault for making me read *Catcher in the Rye*, but I was just being a shit.

At one of our showers (we were blessed with many showers, and many patient friends who still haven't received thank-you cards; thank you!) our pals contributed their favorite children's books. Classics like *The Little Engine that Could* and *Where the Wild Things Are* were coupled with new stories like *Grandpa Green*, about an elderly man whose forest of plant sculptures provides a kingdom of joy for his numerous grandchildren.

Amidst gurgles, a not-even one-year-old Scottie tried to read classic toddler books. She explained in full-on baby talk how *The Very Hungry Caterpillar* grew into a beautiful butterfly. One of the niftier gifts Scottie received was a boxed set of classic fairy tales. She's familiar with the stories mainly due to Disney's animated films, but she appreciates the differences in the original tales and even points them out ("Sleeping Beauty in dis book has seven fairies and dis one is a little girl fairy who makes her go to sleep"). *Jack and the Beanstalk*, a story to which she keeps returning, provides valuable lessons in treating people with respect and the grim error of taking what isn't yours. The fact that she views the Giant's wife as the hero, and Jack as the villain, fills me with pride. "He needs to say he's sorry for taking dat goose," she reminds me upon our umpteenth reading.

We keep the oral tradition alive and well in our home, particularly at bedtime. After a proper book or two, with the lights turned off and her blue nightlight turned on, Scottie will occasionally request one more story. "Dada, tell me da Scottie story." In an effort to get her to go to sleep, I invented a story in which she starred- *Scottie the Saucer Girl*. The main character, Scottie, owns a magic flying saucer that zips into the sky and whirrs around and around. It takes her under the sea and beyond the stars, to remote locations like the Amazon, the vast Sahara desert, and even far off Legoland. She solves problems using her ingenuity and courage. Then she hops into her friendly saucer and it brings the little adventurer home in time for bed. I vary the adventures depending on what we need her to do at that particular time: going on the potty, brushing her teeth, losing the bobo fett, and wearing clothes to school (as opposed to sans clothes, a practice she's espoused). This has yielded mixed results, mostly positive. But the little wisenheimer is a smarty-pants, and started to catch on. Now she'll milk it for three or four stories. "Tell about Dada and da saucer," she commands. "Now Mama and da saucer." She makes her way through the family, and then progresses to things in her room ala *Anchorman*'s Brick Tamland. "I love lamp."

"Tell me 'bout da door and da saucer. Now da pictures. Now da other pictures. Now da bed. Now da diaper change table."

111

This process can take up to an hour or more. Oh yes. No half-ass here. After she's been placated I give her a kiss and we engage in a final "I love you, thwip" and "good guys and gals." She generally throws out one final effort at prolonging bedtime. "You let me hold da book, Da?" I almost always acquiesce, and the little bookworm snuggles up with her stuffed Mickey Mouse under one arm, and a hardback book under the other. Literary bliss.

***

The Bard of Stratford-Upon-Avon part one: the written word

Every bit the book lover, kids ridiculed me for my reading as much as my pal, "Four Eyes". No joke- the kid wore glasses and read books so he was naturally ostracized by the cooler kids and referred to as "Four Eyes". Funny, I can't remember the kid's name, but I distinctly remember his ludicrous nickname. Anyway, we both shared the same cruel fate of ridicule. Because reading was never cool. And no author I read was as uncool to my peers as Shakespeare.

Dad was an actor in addition to being an English teacher, and on both counts he strongly advocated the collected works of one William Shakespeare. Stumbling through the multitude of boxes in a storage closet (Dad was a hoarder), I found his script for a production of *Julius Caesar*. Blocking and character notes, which I emulate closely to this day, were scrawled in the margins and his scansion (marking accents and syllables) painted over the text making it difficult (for me) to read. His

role was that of conspirator and Caesar's most trusted lieutenant, Marcus

Brutus. I was probably seven or eight when I sat down with this precious

artifact. Now I didn't ask Dad's permission; in fact the thought hadn't

even crossed my mind. I was too taken with the text. Here was language

that I'd never encountered on my literary journey. While familiar with

poetry and various metric forms (though I was unaware of my trochees,

spondees, and the like), this author pulled me in with language and with

character.

My most indelible memory of the play remains Marc Antony's

cunning speech to the masses. He's just looked upon the body of his

mentor, his friend, bloodied and lying in the dirt. The murderers, having

won the support of the people, size him up. Will he stand with them? Or

does he need to be dealt with, here and now? Antony convinces them

he'll not interfere, but then uses his wits to carefully sway the crowd to

his side. On the heels of a rousing speech by Brutus, Antony begins:

Friends, Romans, countrymen, lend me your ears;

I come to bury Caesar, not to praise him.

The evil that men do lives after them.

The good is oft interred within their bones;

So let it be with Caesar. The noble Brutus

Hath told you Caesar was ambitious:

If it were so, it was a grievous fault,

And grievously hath Caesar answer'd it.

Here, under leave of Brutus and the rest--

For Brutus is an honorable man;

So are they all, all honorable men--

Come I to speak in Caesar's funeral.

Antony slowly turns the people against Brutus and the conspirators, using the word "honorable" repeatedly to imply the reverse. Despite the language, which I didn't fully understand, comprehension still came. Incredibly, Antony used persuasive speech to completely flip the crowd's loyalties! In his words, "woe to the hand that shed this costly blood!" From then on, Shakespeare had me in his estimable grip.

While Shakespeare's work is brilliant literature, I agree with my college professor, Mary Beth, who would cry during readings from *King Lear* and insist that the power of Shakespeare lies in the *performance* of his work. Most classes she'd force everyone (English majors, especially) to read the works out loud, along with some improv staging. As such, I'll address the poet a bit more extensively in the next chapter, **Theatricality**.

In terms of storytelling, Shakespeare's plays remain accessible to all, despite an existing stigma to the contrary. Scottie was drawn toward my *Collected Works of Shakespeare* (Bevington edition) mainly because of its hefty size. I explained to her that the man who wrote the book was one of Daddy's most influential writers. She asked if we could read it, and I happily obliged. We plowed into the teenage love of *Romeo and Juliet*, and I even tried a bit of the magical isle in *The Tempest*, but her most-loved to this day is *A Midsummer Night's Dream*. Her favorite character was Bottom and, as with any books we read, she preferred each character to have a unique voice. She can't get enough of Bottom, especially when he's turned into a donkey. "Silly Bottom!" she would squeal. "He wants to go back to his friends, but dey are *scaried* (her version of "scared") of him. Dey need to know he's dere friend. Da fairy needs to turn him normal again." She was able to glean all of that simply from the text, without elaboration on my part. Sure, we've had discussions about what transpires, but the text, so well written, tells her what she needs to know.

Scottie's go-to joke for a time was to repeat a Shakespearean phrase (Lady Macbeth's "out damned spot" or Romeo's "but soft, what light through yonder window breaks") and then proclaim "dat's Shakespeare! Shakespeare... apple!" followed by a guffaw. Get it? Your guess is as good as mine.

In 2005, the BBC released a series called *Shakespeare: the Animated Tales* that features condensed versions of the classics voiced by leading members of the Royal Shakespeare Company and other notable Brits. They're all top-notch, but Scottie repeatedly watches

Midsummer and a beautiful stop-motion animated *The Tempest*. Again, accessibility proves key and the BBC has done a fantastic job with these polished and diverse pieces.

The stigma that Shakespeare is too posh or high-falutin' to understand is something we hope Scottie and her generation will break. I feel it's incumbent on those of us older folk not to perpetuate this stigma. Geeks especially- come on! David Tennant played Hamlet and Benedick beautifully. Surely that lends the Bard some geek cred?

***

Sci-fi, fantasy, and young adult novels become cool

I'd pin that coolness on *Harry Potter*, though even that isn't as widespread cool as recent additions to the young adult genre (itself comprised of many subgenres). Today's global community rapidly consumes young adult novels dealing with fantasy creatures, tales of magic and Muggles, and dystopian societies glimpsed years prior in Orwell's *1984*, Huxley's *Brave New World*, and Bradbury's *Fahrenheit 451*.

Harry Potter contemporized magic, and introduced a bevy of fantastic creatures and characters, all against the backdrop of a school setting-- the primary reason, perhaps, for its success. Young adult novels must appeal to, well, young adults, and youthful heroes are the stepping-stones into many of these fabricated worlds (again, DC used this technique with the Batman comics when they introduced Robin).When she was 11 (mirroring the first year a young wizard begins formal training), my little sister-in-law sojourned at midnight with her father to purchase the first book in the Harry Potter series, *The Sorcerer's Stone* (or *The Philosopher's Stone* for my UK friends), and she continued the tradition through to the seventh and final book in the series. Struggles of poor orphaned Harry reinforce one of the most successful themes of young adult literature: how to cope with feelings of isolation during the battle to find your place in the world. Other series landed well in the eighties and nineties (*Artemis Fowl*, Lemony Snicket's *A Series of Unfortunate Events*, and *The Spiderwick Chronicles*), but Harry Potter connected with children and adults in a way not seen in my lifetime since the work of Roald Dahl.

Roald Dahl's worlds captivated me, both as a child and as a parent. In my day his diverse and engrossing stories appealed to all ages. Sure I enjoyed Beverly Cleary and Judy Blume, but as far as children's books went, Dahl was *it* for me. I was head over heels for *The Witches* and *Charlie and the Chocolate Factory*, while Dad preferred its sequel *Charlie and the Great Glass Elevator*. Mom thrilled to the exploits of *The Fantastic Mr. Fox*, and our second grade teacher, the lovely Ms. Sexton, told us how she and her husband wished they could float over the ocean blue with *James and the Giant Peach*.

Charlie's plight, like in any good story, married elements both ordinary and fantastic; while I've never starved or witnessed a gum chewer morph into a blueberry, I connected with Charlie. He was picked on at school, and felt like he was alone. At times, both of those were true of me. He had a loving family. Check. And there were the qualities I aspired to attain: optimism, courage, and faith. That's Charlie Bucket, in a candy wrapper.

Kids and adults today have latched onto newer, and in many cases "edgier", heroes. *Percy Jackson* and his angst-ridden demigod friends deal with the beasts and burdens of Greek mythology. *Twilight* centers around angsty vampires. That's all I care to know about that one. And the biggest craze (as I write this)- *The Hunger Games*. The world over seems ravenous for Young Adult work. And if the entire world (a generalization, granted, but an apt one) is gaga for this science fiction tale it couldn't possibly be considered geeky, right? I mean, the books have sold over 30 million copies (NY Times Bestseller list for three years, and author Suzanne Collins is the bestselling author of all time on Amazon's Kindle), and the film adaptation has hauled in a mighty $155 million-- the best U.S. opening weekend of all time for a non-sequel. Plus kids are now loading up on archery supplies so they can become the next Katniss, and we all know archery is cool.

The point is, when I was reading *Battle Royale*, a Japanese story incredibly similar to *Hunger Games*, it was only cool to gab about it with my friends, and this was when I was out of college! Any time I discussed it, the reaction was something akin to "Ewww, kids killing kids? Who wants to read that geeky crap?" The amazing thing is that I went into *Hunger Games* expecting it to be a lighter version of the brutality in *Battle Royale*, but the violence is much more extreme than I anticipated. I probably wouldn't let my daughter read about kids getting blown up and skewered until she's at least in high school. Of course, I say that now...

We haven't read the *Harry Potter* series to Scottie, as some elements in the latter books are pretty intense. But we'll probably have started on Book One by the time you read this (I might even start tonight). She hasn't expressed interest, though she certainly loves the franchise and its films. The prospect of "chapter books" tantalizes the kid.

Young adult novels carry so much cachet that Hollywood studios hungrily devour the movie rights to any and all stories. Hollywood has even gone back in time to mine geeky fantasy and science-fiction romps with wonderful (*Lord of the Rings*) and not-so wonderful (*John Carter*, while not awful, was a passionate mess) results.

I look forward to Scottie discovering all these worlds independently as well. There was no limit to the places I could go once I started using the library. Dad made a big deal out of me getting my own library card, as it not only meant I'd stop using his, but I was also able to sign my own name. I was six, and my cursive wasn't the greatest but that big blue library card was all mine. Our neighborhood branch was within walking distance from our house. I thrilled at being able to check out whatever I wanted, whenever I wanted. It became bothersome, however, when I wanted to check out a book and it wasn't available. I asked the librarian if I could go to the person's house that checked out Beverly Cleary's *The Mouse and the Motorcycle*, and persuade them to finish the darn thing so I could take a crack at it.

A solution presented itself while Dad shopped for pretzels and cough medicine. I stumbled upon cheapo classics at Walgreens, a store that also happened to be close to my house (once you took the shortcut over the fence, through the ditch, scraping the tunnel, plowing through the tennis courts, skipping through the puddles in the arroyo, and finally across San Mateo boulevard to everyone's favorite drug store/place to buy everything). They had 50 cent books, and I believe my first trip yielded H.G. Wells' *War of the Worlds* and Twain's *A Connecticut Yankee in King Arthur's Court*. Over the years, I think I shifted away from the library and toward Walgreens, because a chance to own my favorite characters' exploits for posterity was far more appealing than borrowing a book for two weeks.

Scottie wants to go to the library, and we haven't been yet. I know, I know- atrocious parenting (but you figured that out three pages in). In the movie version of *Matilda* (we just started the book), self-sufficient little Matilda takes it upon herself to trek across town and visit the library. Scottie pointed to the lavish children's library, and to Matilda's comfy chair in said library, and nodded her head: "Yep, Dad, I want to go dere." Though I'm excited, I temper it with a bit of caution. She's pretty good with books, though she has torn a few pages. She brings me the remnants, asking if I can fix the book for her. There's remorse, and it's one behavior she's definitely improved. Now the danger is a wrinkled book, since she keeps them under her pillow. I've found fewer things bring me as much joy as turning off her reading light after the little tyke has fallen asleep with a book over her head.

School is one place where Scottie has forged her own way, much to our delight. The kids going into kindergarten have a book club where they bring a book from home and share the story with each other. Younger kids aren't excluded, they're invited to attend, but they generally do their own thing when Book Club meets. Apparently the first rule of *their* Book Club is "do your own thing." After a couple sessions, Scottie decided she wanted to butt in on the action. Welcome to Scottie's Book Club. For her first selection, she brought in *Penny Loves Pink*, an Easter present plucked from her Grandma's insanely large gift basket/box. Thanks Mom.

Precocious Penny revels in anything pink, but fails to notice the subtle shift to blue happening around her. She discovers that her parents are having a baby boy, and while initially reticent ("boys are blue!"), she eventually wraps herself in the joy of being a big sister.

Scottie has the book memorized, so it appears she can read it (and I think word recognition has set in; the kid knows her alphabet). Her teachers were stunned by her reading ability, and since Scottie won't go on the toilet, drink out of a cup, or go to sleep without her bobo fett, I'm fine with the teachers touting her as the next Norman Mailer.

The kid spends quite a bit of time with her Grandpa Smith's most beloved author, Mark Twain. It's true. Outside of our bank, there's a bronzed statue of the man sitting on a bench reading *The Adventures of Huckleberry Finn*. Scottie takes it upon herself (after asking his permission, of course) to plop onto the statue's lap and hear the tales of that rascally Huck. To be clear, I haven't read the book to her, but I give a sort of cliff notes and mashed-up version of Huck and Tom Sawyer, with particular slant toward Becky Thatcher in the first volume. This session often concludes with a quick hug and a request for pancakes at the nearby IHOP. I oblige my little bookworm almost every single time, and break out the books I've inevitably brought with me. Scottie can't indulge in flapjacks without slapping *Fancy Nancy* up on the table next to her maple syrup.

6: Theatricality

I'll start by making something clear- theatre, as a vocation, is incredibly difficult. Anybody who says differently is selling something (to quote *The Princess Bride*'s Westley). The notion that being an actor and being a "star" are one and the same is an understandable misconception. However, it *is* a misconception. The reality brings hardship, untold stress, and as much uncertainty as *your* profession, I'd wager. The day I decided to audition for *Peter Pan* (at seven) was one of Dad's proudest days. But he never wanted me to act for a living. That said, nothing career-wise has brought me as much joy as theatre (and it's a close second to being a family man).

Dad was an Educator first and foremost, but he excelled in the second career (he insisted it was a hobby) of acting. As such, I grew up in the theatre, going to rehearsals with him and watching nearly every performance where possible. I think I was seven when Dad did *Guys and Dolls* (his third time) and I witnessed somewhere in the neighborhood of thirty performances. I sat everywhere in that theatre, and was particularly inclined to situate myself nearly on the stage; especially during the Adelaide and the Hot Box Girls dance numbers. My earliest leanings toward the craft (man that sounds pretentious, but it *is absolutely a craft*) occurred during this process. I recorded my version of the entire show, using what we elderly refer to as a "tape recorder". I joke, but some of you reading this may not actually know what that is. Not a problem. I then called Mom on a rotary phone (ours was red, like the Batphone) and told her what I'd done. I performed all the voices, and all the instruments, using my interpretation of the lyrics: "well-heeled shooters" became "well-hid shooters" and so on. I blame it on some of the performers' diction.

Dad and I were leaving his rehearsal of *Light Up the Sky* at the Albuquerque Little Theatre, when I saw an audition notice for *Peter Pan*. To Dad's surprise, I asked if I could go audition. He agreed and we trudged upstairs to the theatre's second space. Thankfully I didn't have to prepare a monologue or anything, since this was a completely impromptu decision. We were given Lost Boys sides to cold read (sides are script pages, cold read means just that, and no I won't make a Kiefer Sutherland joke). I think mine contained the line "I don't know what a *checkbook* is, but..." Following the italicized word, I laid into it and stressed the hell out of it. Dad thought my take was hilarious, and everyone else thought it was... fine. Fine enough to be cast, but it was not to be. Mom refused because of the hours and rehearsal schedule (and strife with Dad), and she had custody of me at the time.

I wasn't deterred by this, and continued to plow forward on my acting path. Mom eventually relented. Some of my earliest roles were as a workhouse boy/Fagin's gang hooligan in *Oliver* (I slipped and flipped over the railing during "Be Back Soon") and as Billy Ray in *On Golden Pond* (I got to say "bullshit" on stage and I loved it). The acting bug struck, and stuck.

While Mom and Pops were initially resistant to this hobby (later profession), I think that had more to do with the animosity between them and Dad than with the actual practice of theatre (if I'm not mistaken, Mom appeared in a production of *Hot L. Baltimore* when she and Dad were married). They mellowed in this stance from about high school on.

Middle school theatre class was great, and also the first time I'd actually gotten to study theatre seriously. I was fortunate enough to have an engaging teacher who opened our first class by reciting Poe's *The Tell-Tale Heart*. She glowered at us as she described the thumping of a buried heart. It was thrilling and totally geeky. And every student (even the occasional jock who signed up because he thought it was an easy class or a great way to get chicks) dove into the deep end with her.

Folks picked on me slightly in mid-school, though less for being in theatre than for all my other pursuits. I did anger a bully on the basketball court as I stood my ground and called a charging foul on him as he plowed into me. A stickler for the rules, am I.

Conflict, I would later learn, is the essence of drama. And perfect fodder for improvisation exercises, my first foray into the subject and theatre as storytelling. Our mid-school improv exercises were lifted from Viola Spolin's textbooks and were incredibly fun to perform. Even the cool kids couldn't deny the power of "Hitchhiker", an improv game wherein a car's inhabitants (on chairs) have to adopt the personality/mannerisms of a picked up passenger. Crocodile Dundee and a person with horrible eczema were two top-tier choices in our group.

High school brought with it many more shows and a bit more acceptance, yet qualities that made me an oddity to the geeks as well as the norms. One of the best examples occurred during my senior year. I'd done sports throughout the years, but was always looked at as a nerdy oddball who happened to be fairly athletic. Despite brief brushes with football my freshman and sophomore years, it was as a senior that I decided to get focused and go out for the Track and Field team. I wanted to throw discus, and did a bit of that, but found true passion and prowess in throwing the javelin. Of all the field events I could've picked, javelin might have been the geekiest. I felt like Achilles taking on the Trojans. It was awesome.

At the same time, I was still in theatre with my friends and getting grief for wanting to keep up with athletic endeavors. I remember having to hurriedly apply old-age makeup to a girl for our production of *The Effect of Gamma Rays on Man-in-the-Moon Marigolds*, because we had to board buses for a track meet in the Heights. My stage manager was upset I couldn't be in the show, and my coaches were bummed I wasn't focused fully on javelin. While still respected by both sides, I never felt fully accepted. People weren't mean to me anymore, but there was always a bit of distance. High school, at times, felt to me like the Marvel Universe, and I was the Watcher- destined to observe, but never to interfere.

An opportunity presented itself in high school to start the process of applying for West Point. Dad had been in the Army during the Korean War (as a medic in Germany, where he played basketball with recuperating soldiers). I suppose I still thought of theatre as a hobby or secondary career- I was positive I'd be an FBI Agent or something like that. The more we got into it, the more I knew that it wasn't for me. I passed the physical, went through all the written stuff, and had gotten recommendations from a Congressman and Senator. But when my West Point liaison tried to con me with "yeah, you can still do theatre- we have a great theatre department!" I decided to call it quits. Dad understood, and supported the decision. I think he was a little saddened, however, as I would have been well taken care of in my career and finances.

Acting was what I had decided to do, and being heavily influenced by Shakespeare I wanted to study on the man's home soil-- the Royal Academy of Dramatic Art (RADA) was where I would hang my hat. Before I even got a chance to start the application process, Dad's cancer came back with sound and fury. He still wanted me to head to the UK, but there was no way in hell I could leave him. As altruistic as that sounds, it was actually a tad selfish. He was my best friend, and I didn't want to be without him.

I always knew playwriting would be an avenue I wanted to explore, and was looking at staying in state once I found out Dad's cancer had returned. I considered heading down south to Las Cruces and New Mexico State University, the home to playwright Mark Medoff (I saw *When You Comin' Back, Red Ryder?* at the NM Rep when I was far younger than the material warranted). You probably know Mark Medoff's *Children of a Lesser God*, which made Marlee Matlin the youngest Lead Actress Oscar winner, and the only deaf one. Medoff can write, and I wanted to glean what I could from him. But he and the University were hours away in Las Cruces.

The main attraction of the University of New Mexico was that I'd get to stay in town with Dad. The added bonus was getting to study under my eventual writing mentor, Digby Wolfe, who spent many seasons as an Emmy winning writer on sketch show *Laugh-In*. Combine that with the steady diet of Woody Allen and Benny Hill on which I was raised, and Digby's teaching style absolutely fit my sensibilities. I was accepted, and relieved to be able to remain in Albuquerque.

I had entertained throwing javelin at the collegiate level, and was approached by the Track and Field coach about it, but I decided to focus on my studies. What started as a double major in Spanish and Criminology (I wanted to be an FBI agent, remember) and minor in Theatre evolved into a major in Theatre with fancy concentrations of Acting and Dramatic Writing, and an almost-minor in Photography (I need one more class to complete the minor, though let's be practical- that ain't gonna happen).

College theatre is incredibly isolating, but I would argue that most of the college experience is as well. You're in the same building for the majority of your university years. Though electives in other disciplines could take you outside your regular environment, there isn't much socialization with those in the daylight. The vast majority of our electives were in the theatre complex. I took as many electives as possible outside the department (I had few available slots), but even our classrooms were located on the basement level of the theatre complex.

At the college level, I was amazed to discover the stigma attached to theatre folks by other departments. My Psychology teacher (an essential class for artists, I believe) expected me to show up late, and a Criminology professor wondered how I remembered "all those lines." To be fair, the guy at the helm of our Western Civilization class loved theatre, and was willing to extend (indefinitely) our papers on Sumerians and such.

The total immersion into theatre history, study, and practice sparked in me a new responsibility to the art. Theatre was always something I enjoyed, but college gave me the vocabulary necessary to take my craft to the next level. It was also there that I met Digby. Digby was this longhaired British guy whose sense of humor remarkably gelled with my sensibilities. I miss him terribly.

My freshman acting teacher, Paul Ford, relished language and his classes were the most stereotypical, yet excellent, touchy-feely courses in my entire college experience. We'd lie on the floor, pretending we were mythological creatures or some such exercise. We learned tongue twisters like "Thetis wrote a treatise noting wheat is silver like the sea" and I loved it. All of this training prepared me for a professional career, though admittedly I wish I'd applied myself even more to my studies. If I had it to do over, I would probably have a little less of a social calendar…

College provided many cool options for study during the summer, including a Shakespeare study abroad, but I unfortunately worked through most of them. When the chance arose to head to Alaska for the Prince William Sound Theatre Conference, I knew I needed to jump on it. Not only had I never been to Alaska, but the guest of honor was Arthur Miller. After one dinner, I found myself in the chilled

Alaskan air alone with the man. We talked about fishing and photography. I mentioned that *Death of a Salesman* and *All My Sons* were two of my favorite plays. "Most people say *The Crucible*," he mused. And instead of leaving it there, I had to be a jackass and tell him it wasn't my cup of tea. The man was gracious, and even chuckled a bit. Then his wife, photographer Inge Morath, pulled up in a company car to give him a lift back to the hotel. It was surreal, and indicative of how many opportunities one is afforded at university. Take advantage of as many as you can, my friend.

My first job out of college was for a theatre where I made the princely sum of $166 a week. FYI- back in "those days" that was still not a lot of money. It didn't matter to me- I was a *paid actor*, and this was definitely my career path. But it made for many hard years (that still continue). Did I want that life for my kids? Not particularly. But the rewards outweighed the trials for me.

Being an actor and a writer enables you to research a variety of topics. The theatrical craft gives its practitioners an eclectic understanding of the world, however cursory that understanding might be. You inhabit human beings through observation, develop a compassion for humanity, and cultivate a better understanding of why people do what they do. Fine rewards, indeed.

***

Scottie loves theatre: 'yay' and 'oh no'

Scottie's theatricality presented itself in the womb; at least that's how I interpret her behavior while slogging it out in her mother's stomach. Look at the evidence- she'd become active whenever we sang to her, Colleen's dancing brought about kicks and punches, and while reading *The Winter's Tale* to Colleen's tummy I swear I felt Scottie's little hand reach out in grand gesture.

As mentioned earlier, she was already well acquainted with theatre having been a captive audience to *Hello Dolly!* and a David Mamet adaptation of Granville-Barker's *The Voysey Inheritance*. As such, I'll focus on her post-womb life literally treading the boards.

Colleen choreographed our annual Christmas show (aptly titled *An American Christmas*) and the fact that Scottie wasn't even 2 months old did nothing to set her off course. Since I was in the show, and our babysitting options were limited, Colleen brought the wee babe to rehearsals with us. She'd sit in a sling across her mother's tummy while Colleen worked through the waltz and a boisterous barn dance. The kid seemed to enjoy this, and would poke her little head out long enough to see me twirling my dance partner (normally Colleen). Satisfied, she'd tuck back into the comfort of the sling.

A few months later, Colleen assistant directed the play *Room Service* (the Marx Brothers made a flick out of it), in which I played a nebbish hotel manager. Scottie sort of assistant assistant directed the piece, crawling around on the stage while pointing and "ba ba ba"ing us, which we took to mean, "pick up the pace, folks." During that same production, she even managed to squeeze her way into the 2009 company photo while sitting on Colleen's lap.

We've spent many years at Lamb's Players Theatre, and I think Scottie will always remember her time there. Colleen headed up our Summer Drama Camps, and since both of us taught there, Scottie graciously agreed to join us (again, babysitting ain't cheap). One of our former students babysat her in the adjacent rehearsal hall/dressing room, but she liked to wander over and see what "da big kids" were up to. This included watching the final dance number for our high schoolers' showcase ("Why We Tell the Story" from *Once on this Island*), applauding, then demanding, "You do da dance again! Please." During one session, another teacher/pal brought Hudson, the young man who coined the "weewok" term. We were doing *The Music Man* at the time and Scottie and Hudson slammed around on the set. We expressed how important it was for them to be careful but hey- they're kids. Scottie, aka Captain Take Charge, grabbed Hudson's hand and moved him ceremoniously up to a platform. The kid used one of her two volumes (loud and exceedingly loud):"Ladies and gentlemen, for boys and for girls, we are married." Hudson was a good sport, and smiled through the proceedings. My daughter seemed serious. No smile. No giggle. Clearly marriage was a sacred institution to Scottie, and we don't smile during a marriage. Apparently.

The marital union quickly forgotten (she says classmate Delaney's brother Tyler is the one for her) she and Hudson continued to romp around the theatre as if it were a Gymboree. Both of them were introduced to the theatre at such early ages that its physical space provided a noticeable comfort to them. Scottie wandered in and out of the green room, waving to folks as she made her way up front to the box office and theatre café. This ease with the stage translated into an appearance in *An American Christmas* when she was a little over one. Set one hundred years in the past, the show features a five-course meal, song, dance, and some scripted segments. That particular year Colleen and I were mushers from Alaska, so Scottie became our little Denali Sunshine (I think I was Gavin and Colleen was Sonoma). Decked out in heavy and hot fur coats and hats, we'd make our mock disruptive entrance as family members arriving late, and Scottie would wave at all the tables. She'd turn and point at the decked-out Christmas tree, begging, "Ball? Ball!" Sticking a cute kid in a Christmas show guarantees "awww"s.

A few years later our friends' daughter Madeline appeared in the theatre's other Christmas offering, *Festival of Christmas*, and stole the show during her brief appearance at the finale. Colleen directed it and initially wanted Scottie for an expanded role, but I wasn't keen on bedtime getting out of whack. Any deviation, and Scottie assumes she can push for anything ("I want da Chicken Mickeys in bed and my bobo fett and I don't wanna go to bed- not ever"). So her second stage appearance didn't happen there. It happened at her pre-school.

We dig Scottie's school for many reasons, not the least of which are the "Music with Betty" days. The delightful Betty brings in instruments and stories, teaching the kids the musicality of language and sound. In the weeks leading up to Christmas, Betty and Scottie's wonderful teachers, Michelle and Grace, prepped the kids to perform excerpts from *The Nutcracker*. Scottie's Seedlings galloped around as… flowers, I think? I'm not entirely sure, but Scottie did a nifty lunge maneuver center stage and waved her wand around in an attempt to replicate the dance moves. The performance ended with all the kids, led by Betty, singing a nifty song: "sing, sing, sing Shalom, sing Shalom together" and other cultural/linguistic iterations. As everyone filtered into the hallway for a cookies and cupcakes reception, Scottie wandered back to center stage and wondered aloud "Where's everybody going? We still going to do da show? Hey everybody! Come back! Come baaaaaaaaaaack!"

With her comfort on stage (despite having anxiety in certain avenues) we devised a gift-buying plan of puppets, culminating in Santa bringing her a stand-up puppet theatre. Her aforementioned fascination with the Muppets has fueled her desire to create shows, which range from a Snow White puppet making pancakes, to Shakespeare begging a shark to escort him to the movies. When she's misplaced her puppets (probably under the couch), she uses her hands for the characters. She tells us, as her audience, to please turn off our cell phones and not to talk.

Etiquette is at the forefront of Scottie's theatre education, and the majority of it is self-imposed. She's been to many children's theatre productions, theme park shows (she behaves as if she's in a theatre), and dress rehearsals for "big people" shows. During each of these she sits, hands clasped, offering applause and laughter where she deems necessary. This past December, we attended *The Grinch* at The Old Globe, an overlong adaptation of the Dr. Seuss classic. She was fantastic, but you could see when she became disconnected from the material. She maintained her poise, however, if not her interest. Ironically, an usher approached me to put my phone away twenty minutes before the show. I was texting my babysitter and needed to confirm a schedule with her following the performance. Stifling my desire to tell her I was the last person in the world she had to worry about, I said "of course" and stowed the phone. Scottie reminded me that phones in the theatre are a no-no, and I assured her that I wouldn't call anybody while in the auditorium, nor would it be present for the show. Satisfied, she patted my hand and perused her program.

Speaking of Mr. Geisel (a longtime La Jolla resident), Colleen, Scottie, and I had the pleasure of going to a youth theatre production of *Seussical* on Dr. Seuss' birthday. Again the flawless audience member, she let loose a bit when the Circus McGurkus appeared, hooting and hollering for the specialty acts. She then whispered, "We have to be quiet in da feater, Mama and Dada" and patted us both as if we were the offenders. She treats movie theatres like theatrical venues in this regard, and maintains the same courtesy she would when attending a live stage show. Would that modern audiences follow her example. Oy.

Recently my little ham discovered accents. Her favorite is Standard British, and she pronounces her double Ts like *th*, i.e. Harry Potter becomes Harry Po*th*er. She emulates Catherine Tate in *Doctor Who*, picking up a phone receiver and heatedly questioning, "You had the reception wifout me?" Last night in the bath we had an entire dialect coaching session. Scottie had set up a floating tea party, using the aforementioned *Bath Time* book as a tray, and she intoned "would you like thum mo tea, Daddy?" Her lispy interpretation of British speech in full effect, I asked her to watch my mouth as I formed the words. She stuck her tongue back in her mouth, and mimicked my speech perfectly. "Pinky up, Daddy." Apparently this goes with the accent.

***

The Bard of Stratford-Upon-Avon part deux: the acted word

During LPT's Summer Drama Academy, it was my pleasure to head up the Shakespeare instruction. The last year I did it, I showed up armed with my Bevington edition of *The Collected Works*, two volumes of Shakespearean lexicon, and a giant post-it pad. Stepping onto stage to face the students, I mentioned that it was time to bust out some Shakespeare. Resounding applause. Beat. I fell on my face.

Okay, not really. But I was overwhelmed with the level of enthusiasm. Oh, I'd received sarcastic enthusiasm in the past, snotty "Oh boy!"s, and "wheeee!"s. But this was genuine excitement, and something I'd not experienced at the onset of Shakespearean study.

Normally at the end of a two-week session, the students were completely caught up in Shakespeare's stories. They found, quite rightly, that many of their own experiences were reflected in his plays. As enjoyable as this was, I think I literally wept when chatting about the event with Colleen.

I've already discussed the geek stigma surrounding Shakespeare and theatre; now imagine combining both. Even with Kenneth Branagh making Will's words more accessible, there's still a distancing element that I think can only be conquered through an emphasis on Shakespeare's storytelling. Too often, his language is seen as an obstacle. If we focus on the story and characters, the language becomes a vehicle to take us into the situations. I've seen it happen- a student (child or adult) begins to invest in the drama of the play, and even a casual reader/audience member can grasp that Romeo loves Juliet, yet their love is forbidden by parental and societal standards. Performance is the key; again, the man wrote plays to be seen and heard- not read.

My personal Shakespearean odyssey took years to develop, and of course I'm still on the path of discovery (I will, however, plug my forthcoming Young Adult adventure series *Will's Quills,* which is strongly influenced by the playwright). As mentioned, I was familiar with his work from an early age, yet I hadn't acted out his words in a full production until college. I'd done monologues and scenes all through middle school and high school. But college brought me closer to the Bard.

Kristen Loree's voice and movement class, where we did indeed "suit the action to the word, the word to the action" (*Hamlet's* advice to the players), allowed students to indulge in the language. During lines like "for in the very torrent, tempest and as I may say, whirlwind of your passion" (again, *Hamlet*), we pounded our *T's* and conjured *Wh* whirlwinds with our articulators.

My first college production was in a modern-dress version of *As You Like It* as Orlando's villainous brother, Oliver. The production was ridiculous; it was set at a ski lodge and our Charles the Wrestler looked like the Gimp from *Pulp Fiction*. I myself was attired in thick *Terminator*-esque glasses and a snowboarding jacket. Ridiculous. But I was doing a full Shakespearean show, and I loved it. The dampener to the proceedings was the fact that Dad had been in the hospital with his latest bout of cancer, and he died during my first week of rehearsal (also the first week of college). While devastating, I took a modicum of comfort in the fact that I was able to tell Dad about getting cast, and his tired reaction was simply a smile.

An old friend of Dad's happened to be my high school drama teacher. Mr. M (that's what we called him) taught us out of university Theatre History textbooks, and switched our learning focus to a different avenue of theatre every quarter. By the time we had completed our high school studies, every theatre student had at least some experience as a playwright, stage manager, lighting designer, costumer, director, actor, and many more. We'd learned about Japanese theatrical styles: Bunraku puppet theatre; Noh, a style with emphasis on movement due to the masks the actors wear; and Kabuki, with its extreme gestures and expressive makeup. We studied everything from Greek drama to Sam Shepard. But the first monologue we learned and performed was a classic from Shakespeare. We got to pick from a list, but as soon as I read "Friends, Romans..." at the top of the page, I made my choice.

Even among the theatre crowd, those of us that liked

Shakespeare (and there weren't many) were seen as a bit odd. We weren't

excluded; we were simply curiosities. As with most theatre (and art in

general, it could be argued), companies employ "name" actors in an

attempt to draw in audiences. In addition to the aforementioned David

Tennant versions of *Hamlet* and *Much Ado About Nothing*, stage and

screen have utilized the talents of Maggie Smith (Professor

McGonagall), Ian Mckellan (Magneto and Gandalf), and Patrick Stewart

(Captain Picard and Professor X)... notice a trend? Geeks and normies

alike respond to the characters these actors have played, and that makes

them ideal candidates to bring Shakespeare to a broader audience. Their

extensive stage credits don't hurt, either. Kenneth Branagh was able to

use training and skills honed at the Royal Shakespeare Company to

cement his status as the contemporary Shakespeare-on-film guy (though

Julie Taymor has added her stamp to Shakespeare with her films *Titus*

and *The Tempest*).

Branagh's first foray into the cinematic world of William

Shakespeare was the epic *Henry V* in 1989 (the same year as Tim

Burton's *Batman*). Since then he's produced many more, with mixed

results. *Love's Labours Lost* ranks as the lamest attempt on record to get

into Alicia Silverstone's pants. Though I do have to give credit to

Branagh for a third of Marvel's *Thor* movie (he gets an A for the

Asgardian portion of the tale, while the earth-bound stuff left me weary).

Shakespeare in Love, besides winning multiple Oscars, legitimized Shakespeare for the mainstream. I saw it with a group whose members had varying experience with Shakespeare. The least-versed in Shakespeare (that is to say, she had no experience with his work) adored the film. The latest cinematic journey into the Shakespeare mythos, *Anonymous*, fared quite poorly. Perhaps because it dared question whether Shakespeare actually wrote the works to which he's attributed, or if it was in fact the Earl of Oxford, Edward de Vere who lent his quill to the task. Or perhaps it failed because the film was directed by the guy who brought us *The Day After Tomorrow* and *2012* (his *Independence Day* remains a guilty pleasure of mine).

My journey to the UK yielded very little when it came to Shakespeare research. This was mainly due to the fact that when we weren't rehearsing, we were in pubs close to our lodgings. I'm curious to see what England thinks of its most famous writer. There couldn't possibly exist the stigma that Shakespeare is stuffy and posh, could there? It's something I'll definitely explore on future trips abroad.

On the horizon, Colleen will be directing a musical version of *A Midsummer Night's Dream* for one of San Diego's newest theatrical offerings, Intrepid Shakespeare Company. Out of necessity, Scottie will have to attend a large portion of the rehearsals, and I'm energized at the prospect of immersion into her favorite of Shakespeare's works. The Artistic Directors of the classically-bent company have a new baby boy, who will be brought up around William Shakespeare and Henrik Ibsen, Arthur Miller and Henry James, and that alone gives me hope for the next generation. Go geeks.

Why Shakespeare over, say, Kyd or Marlowe? What is it about the way he chose to express his world; the syntax he chose, and the intention of his drama? I think it's the way his language propels the action like no other classical author I'd read. While poetic, it's *dramatic* poetry that characters use to accomplish their goals. George Carlin said the one true power we have as humans is the ability to carefully choose our words. It's a power we don't always exercise- Shakespeare perfected that power.

***

Theatre is vital.

Sure, but why? Folks more eloquent than I have written plenty of books on the subject, so I don't want to answer that for you. All I ask is that you sit in the audience of a solid piece of theatre and experience the joy of connecting in an arena where your gasps, your laughter, and your applause impact an unspoken conversation you're having with your fellow audience members and the actors. That's easier said than done, unfortunately, due to the abundance of sub-par theatre companies operating. Even these, I would offer, have the opportunity to resonate with *somebody*, even though it might not be your particular mug of butterbeer. The object is simply to connect, to extend those dendrites.

Taking theatre as a kid gave me a support beam that has withstood earthquakes and hurricanes, and days both dark and light. Geeky outcasts find solace in one another, really no different from athletes bonding together in team sports. We observed the power of theatre to start a very immediate, very real, human conversation that anyone had the power in which to partake.

Theatre is synonymous with being, in the sense that its practitioners attempt to observe humanity and replicate that observation through the filter of their own experiences. Good theatre amplifies a common feeling, and shows us a truth we recognize in an acquaintance or in ourselves.

I joke about wanting but not wanting Scottie to follow in our footsteps. There is truth in both angles. Nothing would make me happier than sitting in on her many opening nights, flowers in hand. But the hardship of the profession is something I've experienced for the majority of my professional career. Nonprofit theatre, like most other nonprofits, has been in a crisis period for some time, with many esteemed nonprofits closing their doors (notably the Tony award-winning Theatre de la Jeune Lune in Minneapolis). Though I'm relatively stable in theatre terms, I live my life in a kind of bubble- I spend most waking moments analyzing the fragility of that bubble, and devising ways to survive should it burst. I'm in a salaried position, but that offers only slightly more comfort than working freelance. No matter how many projects you line up, you're always waiting for the other shoe to drop. Which is what theatre conditions you for, sadly.

All that said, I want to equip Scottie with every tool necessary to survive any profession, should she choose theatre or rocket science (I'm obviously well-versed in both subjects). With our students, Colleen and I communicate the importance of understanding and appreciating theatre, regardless of your profession. A 2009 study showed that multi-disciplinary arts students outperformed their non-arts peers on the SAT by 91 points. Many studies, many positives for the arts. Many positives for theatre. Even more than these studies, it's the effect I see on students and audiences, practitioners and patrons, that demonstrates to me the magic of telling a worthy story on stage.

One of the more positive things to come out of that production of *The Grinch* was the fact that so many children were introduced to a piece of theatre. As actors we live our lives under the assumption that every show is one audience member's first and another's last. I take the responsibility of that simple assumption seriously. That means no half-assed performances. Do the best you can do every time you set foot on stage. And I take action to spread this application in every aspect of my life. "Action is eloquence," Shakespeare writes in *Coriolanus* (3.2). Damn right, Will. Let's take action.

7: Geeky Outings

Archaeopteryx. Any idea what that is? How about Rhamphorhynchus? I'll give you one more. Tyrannosaurus Rex. Ah yes. *Dinosaurs.* I was obsessed with them, starting around four years of age. Probably why I almost crapped my pants twelve years later upon seeing that Brachiosaur lumber against the skyline in *Jurassic Park.* I knew all their names, all their attributes. If I couldn't ride a Stegosaurus or observe an armor-plated Ankylosaurus swinging its mighty tail, I had to go with the next best thing and that was a trip to the Albuquerque Zoological Society. I'd grab my stuffed monkey Nicky, who was given to me by my older sister Deb when I was a baby, and we'd be off in Dad's Ford Escort EXP (with trendy 80s spoiler).

The Zoo was one of my favorite excursions with Dad, thanks in no small part to the groovy song he invented. "We're going to the zoo, we're going to the zoo. Lancey, and Daddy, and little Nicky too." The man's voice was awful- he performed the old "speak-sing" technique during any musical in which he appeared, but I loved his made-up tunes.

Our Zoo was okay, but the Reptile House was surprisingly immersive. Twists and turns took you deeper into the lizard labyrinth, and I loved it. Dad wasn't ever too keen on reptiles (the only trait he shared with Pops), but he obliged me my excursions into the snake pits. I'd reenact the scene from *Raiders* when Indy stares down the cobra. Most times the cobra was off exhibit, but it didn't stop me from enlisting Dad's aid as Sallah.

While she's not quite the reptile geek I was/am, Scottie was fascinated with the animal kingdom from the get-go. I think our earliest regular excursions as a family were to the world-famous San Diego Zoo, since Colleen's former roomie Renee hooked us up with zoo passes for our wedding (she also gave us the "Rebold spice", a potent concoction that's perfect on popcorn). We pushed Scottie along in her too-big-for-a-weewok stroller, and she'd silently watch the flamingos stroll through the water. When words came, she pointed to the animals on the map she wanted to visit and barked. "Dis one," she'd insist, tapping the monkey icon on the map. The kid communed with the great apes Diane Fosse style, and loved pressing her entire (tiny) body against the glass. The orangutan on exhibit occasionally mirrored this behavior on the other side of the glass, reinforcing Scottie's actions on subsequent visits.

With even more words, came more specific requests. Scottie begged to see "da Harry Potter snake". She referred, of course, to the python from the first film that Harry unwittingly sets free with his Parseltongue and magic powers. It was around this time that she also fixated on elephants. I don't know why the pachyderms were her chosen obsession, but it's a good thing we lived where we did. We had moved to Carlsbad, relatively close to the Wild Animal Park (which is in the wilds of Borneo, apparently). Scottie used her arm as a trunk to "talk" to the giants, and regulars of the facility informed her of each animal's name.

She naturally loved the creatures of the ocean: we live in San Diego, plus I've always wanted to swim with denizens of the sea so apparently it's genetic. I managed to accomplish this feat while working at Sea World (beluga whales were my swimming companions), and Colleen would bring Scottie to take in my shenanigans with sea lions and otters (and the most unpredictable animals: the trainers). While she's enjoyed a few aquariums, Sea World offers her the gamut from penguins to walruses. And Sesame Street characters. I loved taking her there on my off days, and we'd close out the night watching fireworks on the bay from our rickety perch inside the sky buckets.

Outings with my Dad could entail a truck stop visit where I'd walk along the flatbeds of the semi-trucks, or a train ride to Vegas. Las Vegas, New Mexico, that is. We'd head up there for the day and poke around the dusty town, and there was an old-school "arcade" game in a hotel where I'd plunk in a nickel and turn a lever to race metal horses in a case. Quaint though it was, I needed the time with Dad away from my average grind.

I guess I thought every outing with Scottie would fulfill the nostalgic bliss I associated with my childhood excursions. Obviously, this was not to be. A large chunk of Scottie's anxiety (and she still struggles with this today) occurred during the melding of two disparate worlds. Namely when her school life crossed with her family life. She was relatively new to pre-school when we went on a field trip to a pumpkin patch. The school encouraged parents to attend, and Scottie seemed to be in support of the whole thing. Once we hit the waiting area and she saw her classmates playing in the hay bales, she froze. She didn't want to go in and a spectacular meltdown ensued. I carried her around through the beanbag toss, past the mini pumpkin maze, and over to the hay bale pyramid in the middle. "Dis is no good, Dada. No good at all!" I agreed. Her teachers understood, and even offered to give her a lift back, but by that point Scottie hung onto me like an Alien facehugger. We bade farewell to the frivolity and settled in for a long journey home.

This past Christmas we sallied forth on our biggest trip to date: miraculous Orlando, FL. We figured we'd gather the whole extended family and take in not only the various parks in Disneyworld, but also Universal Studios' Islands of Adventure and the crown jewel therein-Harry Potter Land. I like the bespectacled wizard well enough, but Colleen's love borders on fanaticism. All of us enjoyed the park, but as with most excursions, watching the proceedings through the eyes of a three-year-old is magic to rival any of Dumbledore's conjurings. Scottie received the added bonus of hanging out with superheroes at the Marvel Island. She traded quips with Green Goblin ("I can't listen to you cuz you're fwawed, Green Goblin") and showed her patriotism in a salute with Captain America. Storm was fantastic, and took the time to kneel down and talk to Scottie about anything and everything for a solid five minutes. Scottie was in heaven and so were we, though passing through Hogsmeade and into Harry Potter Land elevated all of us (Colleen's Harry Potter lovin' little sister Megan was with us) even higher.

The most packed area in the entire park, Harry Potter Land completely immerses you in the wizarding world. While waiting in an hour and a half line at Olivander's Wand Shop (to witness a short wand selection ceremony) I purchased some pumpkin juice and gabbed with Colleen and Megan (who added humor and some much-needed Scottie-sitting) about all the small details Universal had put into the little village. Scottie didn't care about any of this- she just wanted her wand. She wasn't selected for the mini-show, but she knew her prize resided behind the door that the smiling wizard guarded. The show wrapped up and Scottie sweetly, but forcefully, asked if now was the time we could buy her wand. We did, and the kid now hurls spells around the room (and away from the television) with speed and accuracy. Wand purchase complete, we poked around for my treat: Butterbeer.

Granted the mystical treat was a non-alcoholic cream soda, but it was damn tasty. Colleen, Megan, and I followed up with the real stuff, a draft of amber beer manufactured right there at the Hog's Head (or at Universal's wholesaler). When the waitress returned, Scottie took the lead. "Dada will have da butterbeer," an order she's repeated at many a restaurant to this day. With the amount of people I witnessed ordering butterbeer, in at least five or six languages, I think it safe to say that Harry Potter geekdom knows no borders.

Geeks abound at the geekiest destination event on the planet: the San Diego Comic Con. The affair has expanded (much to my dislike, actually) into every aspect of pop culture, and attendees can now find their favorite comedy TV show next to a booth promoting handmade dolls that look like organs. Celebrities and movie studios have made this a must-stop on their yearly itinerary, and that weirds me out to no end. Thankfully there are plenty of comic book-related items and attractions to satisfy me. One of last year's highlights was a life-size action figure photo-op, where attendees could enter a glass case as the newest action figure in the Avengers Assemble line. Scottie, Colleen, and I each took our turns before moving on to the *Yo Gabba Gabba* booth. Our weewok freaked out because she wanted to meet Brobee and the gang, but they weren't scheduled to appear until later. Wonder Woman, who happened to be nearby, approached her and through the immediate recognition of her garb, was able to instantly calm Scottie down. Flash (my favorite DC character) also assisted and Scottie was inducted as a junior member of the Justice League. By two random fans. That, to me, is what Comic-Con should be about, Charlie Brown. We bought her a Muno stuffed animal, and on the way to our car stopped to take a picture with Wile E. Coyote (next to the Chuck Jones Gallery).

Scottie's a nut for pictures. Any character, no matter how obscure, will suffice. She had no idea who Chuck E Cheese was, but decided that we needed to pay him a visit. When I was her age, Chuck E. Cheese was a gigantic affair. The building itself housed four or five separate areas, one of which was a giant party area with an entire band of animatronic characters and moving creatures on the walls. Their video game selection was immense, and I know my folks spent a pretty penny on many a party.

This particular venue, while entertaining, was a shadow of the pizza parlor I remembered. I really didn't need to spend any money (even though I did), as Scottie seemed content to run around like a lunatic and pretend to play games. She enjoyed the animatronic Chuck (the sole animatronic character in the whole place), and followed a less-than-enthusiastic costumed character on a hunt for tickets. This ended in a photo op, and my kid was one of the first to leap up and pose. She mistook another bald gentleman for me, but eventually found her way back to her O.G. Papa.

A minor freak out occurred when she asked to go in the seemingly hermetically sealed glass case. Kids go in there, strap on a pair of goggles, and attempt to catch as many prize tickets as possible while strong fans blow them all around. She was cool with the goggles, but as soon as the door shut she pressed against the glass, screaming. I saved her and calmed her down with a little pizza and a lot of tokens. There was that anxiety.

Her fear manifests itself most clearly in outings, places with which she's unfamiliar or in which she feels she won't prosper. In quite a few trips, she's been wary of the beach despite yearning to play on the sun-soaked sand. She's also begged me to take her surfing after repeated *Lilo and Stitch* viewings. This is reinforced by *The Daddy Book*, one of our bedtime standards which states "all daddies like to try new things with you" while showing a Dad and kid riding the waves. We're due for another beach trip, so perhaps in an update I'll let you know how it went.

***

Neighborhood excursions

A trip to the park to fly a kite (the kid's a master with her Disney princess kite) or to play on the decrepit playground equipment isn't inherently geeky, but the route we take to get there is. Rounding the corner from our house, we pass the pizza place with the amazing happy hour to stop by the corner bookstore, Adams Avenue Books. I love my

Kindle, but the lure of a locally owned bookstore filled with smelly, tangible books makes me giddy. Scottie gets a trifecta of fun: cats roam free and commune with her (though she did tell a cat "dat's really not nice, cat, you need to apologize" when it hissed at her), she sits reading in an entire room devoted to kids' books, and she and I lounge on the comfy leather chairs in the geography section playing chess and Chinese checkers. Admittedly, she doesn't know how to play either very well (I've tried to teach her, and will continue to do so), but it's an intense affair.

Leaving the bookstore we have the option to stop by either the "Avengers Assemble" toy store (it has Cap, Wolvie, Spidey, and the Hulk painted onto its bright yellow exterior) or swing into the ice cream shop for a treat. I'd say ice cream wins out only slightly over the toy store, but the lure of both is equally strong. The toyshop's proprietor is fantastic, and he even threw in a free mask/ring combo when we bought her some Green Lantern toys. All at her request, I might add. Wonder Woman's lasso of truth.

***

Disneyland and the repeat customers

The advent of annual passes to various amusement parks enables a new level of geekdom. Fans can visit as often as they wish, and memorize every minute detail of the layout. Nowhere is that more prevalent (to me, anyway) than at the happiest place on earth:

Disneyland. I can only speak to SoCal's mouse house since my visits to Disneyworld have occurred twice: this past Christmas with the family, and during my honeymoon with my ex-wife (Hey oh! I won't be getting into that here).

When I first moved to Los Angeles, I decided I needed to revisit the place that had made me so happy as a whippersnapper. I invested in a Disneyland pass, albeit a cheapie resident discount that offered year-round admission but many blackout dates. One visit was all it took to illustrate that as big a Disney fan as I thought I was, I couldn't hold a candle to the die-hards I encountered on my trips. Trying to find my way on a map, I used Sleeping Beauty's castle as a landmark. "Sleeping Beauty Castle. No possessive." I turned to find a pin-clad passholder sizing me up. "That's a common mistake," he informed me. Okay. Over the course of my time as a passholder, both single and now with Colleen and Scottie, we've encountered a hardcore Disney geek on every visit. The interesting thing to me is how each Disney geek seems to specialize in a certain ride or attraction. We happened to ride Scottie's new obsession, the Jungle Cruise, twice in a row. An immediate connection was made with a member of the voyage who rode the jungle cruise for hours on end, daily. She noticed we were on our second trip around, and started geeking out about the self-referential nature of the "guide" and how much cooler the voyage is at night. We nodded, and Scottie told her to watch out for the hippos because "dey're mad wif our boat- see da ears wiggle?" She's well on her way to becoming a Disney geek.

A fellow Disney fan (I can't call us geeks- we'd be left in the dust by some of the people I've met) turned me on to Disneyland apps for the iphone; they divulge the wait times of all the rides, as well as the locations of ludicrously large turkey legs (which are really emu legs, but I digress). The app I use most has a separate message board for Disney geeks to get together and do what geeks of any other obsession do: show off their knowledge.

In all fairness, we each have our own Disney tradition/obsession when visiting the park. I can't leave without swinging by the Tiki Room for a Dole Pineapple Whip Float- fresh pineapple juice topped with pineapple soft serve. Colleen's Disneyland experience isn't complete without a refillable coffee and a peanut butter chunk cookie from the "secret" bakery near Winnie the Pooh's ride. And Scottie's *raison d'etere*: Sleeping Beauty (non-possessive) Castle.

Disneyland remains perhaps our most successful outing destination and besides the inherent allure of the park, I believe it all comes down to the tram ride back to the parking structure. Scottie usually flips out when we leave the park, but there's enough eye candy in Downtown Disney (or *Downton* Disney, as my Brit-loving wife calls it) to keep her occupied until we reach the final "ride." She spies the tram and lights up, excitedly rushing us forward to hop on "da red one, da red one!" More often than not, her excitement quickly fades and the kid crashes out before we hit Disneyland Drive. Another successful day, and one step closer to Starbucks for Mommy and Daddy's drive home. Ah, Starbucks- one of Mommy and Daddy's favorite outings.

8: Princesses and Gender roles

"Vasquez! Pull out left and plug those Aliens full of lead and stuff. Hudson! Swing over the monkey bars and get to the slide. Apone! They're all over! AIYYYYYYYEEEEEE!" Ah, the sounds of fifth graders role-playing on the playground. And those ten- and eleven-year-olds were my friends and I. James Cameron's *Aliens* had just been released and we played out the Colonial Marines' bug hunt during every recess. It made no matter that the film was R-rated; we loved it and we weren't the only ones. Now, to clarify, we WERE the only ones actually role-playing, but certainly the film was a hot topic amongst the students (albeit underground, so adults couldn't chastise us).

The unique aspect of our little band of play soldiers was the lone representative of the fairer sex: good ol' Shannon. A tomboy through and through, there was very little girly-girl about her. We talked up the Lakers/Bulls series, and enjoyed swapping insect bite stories. She swore like a sailor (well, she said 'damn' and 'hell' a lot, at any rate). She wasn't strange at all and, contrary to how cruel kids can be, was heralded by the normie kids as something of a revelation. Even the girls seemed to crave her secret to commanding boys' attention. My geeky bunch saw her as one of the guys, however. Had we but opened our eyes a tiny bit wider, we would have seen a lovely young woman. None of us would've made a move, of course.

Years later (college, to be precise) I bumped into her at my local comic book shop, and there's nothing sexier to a geek than a beautiful woman who knows Marvel from DC. While many may mock this mentality, it's no different for sports fiends when they find a woman who wants to head over to the pub because the Clippers are playing in the NBA Finals (anybody who supports the Clips is aces in my book).

I'm continuously surprised at how we perpetuate gender role stereotypes, and it's irresponsible to place the blame entirely on the media. I do it. I try not to, but I do. On the other hand, how awful is it to introduce princesses to girls and knights to boys? When it came to my religious upbringing, Dad (an atheist, later an agnostic) wanted to make sure I studied as many world religions as possible before making a decision (I was raised by Mom and Pops as a Southern Baptist, but not the cool *Blues Brothers*, flipping in the aisles and dancing to James Brown type). While I appreciated this, and it fits our parenting style to a degree, we don't go full tilt in presenting Scottie with a balanced diet of traditionally male or female points of interest. We try, but we also leave a bit to the winds of fate (i.e. the Internet- KIDDING).

Because I'm her Dad, she naturally latched on to my geeky (and traditionally male) pursuits. Tyrone Power's *Mark of Zorro* was harmless enough and I was fine watching it with an incredibly young Scottie, especially with her ability to make a 'Z' in the air. Superheroes of course factored in, but since Colleen and I both enjoy Disney films we incorporated the Mouse into our movie-watching routine.

We initially attempted to avoid Disney movies, as the majority of fairy-tale princesses were presented as damsels in distress, incapable of getting themselves out of the usually avoidable situations they're in. Female heroes (I refuse to call them heroines because, well, there it is) seem to have gotten bolder as reflected in Ripley from *Aliens* and the more age-appropriate (and recent) Merida from Pixar's *Brave*. Scottie insisted on adding Disney's *Mulan* to our home rotation. *Mulan* is a study in gender politics in and of itself, though I like to think of it as a variation of the 80s gender-bender *Just One of the Guys*. Mulan, attempting to save her father from military conscription, must disguise herself as a man in order to take her father's place. It's been inspiring to see the world through Scottie's eyes, and examining another culture's perception of gender is equally exhilarating. She notes not only the Chinese cultural differences, but also the fact that the story must take place "a long time ago far away from San Diego."

"She has to be a man, but she's a lady," Scottie pieced together. "Why can't she just be a lady, Daddy?" This was where we talked about the cultural and generational differences, and Scottie revealed "well, I'm

Scottie- I'm a little girl and I have a sword too, but I am NOT a boy."

A friend of Mom's generously wanted to make Scottie a baby blanket, and Mom asked what we'd like on it. We were very clear about our desires for an all-Pixar character blanket. *Finding Nemo*, *Toy Story*, and *Monsters Inc.* were a few suggestions we gave. Apparently this translated to Mom as "we want Disney princesses" and as sure as Dopey's grin, we received a beautifully handmade blanket adorned with Ariel and Cinderella, with a center tile reading "FOR OUR LITTLE PRINCESS." Mom assumed Pixar equals Disney, and Disney plus girl equals princess. And hell, she ain't alone. That's certainly what I'd always thought and it wasn't like somebody sat me down and said "you see, Lance, girls are supposed to like these Disney princesses, and you should be into *The Black Cauldron* or *The Sword in the Stone* if you're going to like any Disney movie."

We certainly place no parameters on Scottie's femininity. She takes her cues from us, of course, but the kid likes what she likes. Genre and gender mashups generally occur. Inhabiting Spider-Man is a breeze for the kid, and she asked for the Spidey face paint over all other designs at the Adams Avenue Roots Festival (a street fair that takes up half the city). However, she wanted her princess hair clip holding back her bangs so as not to be blinded during web slinging. She activated her imaginary web-shooters at the same street fair to THWIP! cake from a vendor into mouth.

While surfing through cartoon intros for "girly shows" (*Jem* and *Strawberry Shortcake*), some of YouTube's other suggested videos were the 60s Marvel cartoon intros. These initiated the concept of being able to assume the identity of multiple heroes at once, since she watched every intro back to back. I mentioned her mashup of Snow White/Avengers. An earlier incarnation (when she was about two years old) was Hulk Princess. Simple in design, Hulk Princess consisted of a pair of foam Hulk hands and a raggedy Hawaiian dress. Later, this look evolved into her generic princess/fairy outfit, advantageous in its versatility. The foundation was established for an infinite number of combinations. Fortunately her friends at school, of both sexes, enjoy her imaginative role-playing and follow her on her non-gender specific adventures.

Underneath the stairs we have a little nook that has been designated as the repository for Scottie's toys and books. She likes to play *Wizard of Oz* and turn out the lights as we wander through the haunted forest. We eventually find our way to the nook, which transforms into a giant cave where all of Dorothy's friends hide from the witch. Crouched into this tiny space, we begin our quest to bring the members of the band out of hiding. She has no difficulty assigning me the role of Dorothy, and is likewise eager to become the Lion, Tin Man, or Wicked Witch. The way she looks at it, it's all in service of the narrative.

At school, Scottie shared her love of pirates and sword fighting (and Peter Pan) with her best friend, Claire, and other boy friends (friends who are boys, hence the space- she's not dating till I'm ready for grandkids). I'm a bit more lenient on the sword fighting than Colleen, though I do stress the importance of proper form using imaginary blades. Safety first! For family week, Colleen and I came in and taught a pirate ditty to all the kids. Much to my pleasure every one of them, boys and girls, took to the seven seas with gusto and grit. We swashbuckled around the fenced-in playground, escaping Thomas (the University of San Diego student aide) who swam after us pretending to be a ferocious shark. The kids even humored us by wearing the stick-on mustaches we'd brought for the class.

One of Scottie's teachers recently expressed concern for her well-being. She was playing superheroes with the older boys. Her superhero? Princess Flower Girl (she's obsessed with serving as a flower girl at weddings, despite batting 0-1). Her teacher was afraid that Scottie wouldn't be able to keep up with the boys' aggressive style of play. I'll admit Scottie is a bit of a conundrum- she loves roughhousing, but her anxiety can manifest itself in physical situations. I've witnessed her sling her body fearlessly across a jungle gym, yet freeze when presented with a small slide. What little time I've spent in her class, I've observed Scottie baking in the kitchen with Claire and then running full speed around the bike path with the boys (and into them). I'd like to say we send her to school in cute little dresses and whatnot, but the reality is that her school encourages kids to play in the mud (something we support). So 15% of school days she wears a nifty sundress with cute leggings (when Colleen dresses her). 80% of the time, it's a t-shirt and jeans/shorts (when I dress her). The other 5% is Marty McFly gear. At school, she's never been mistaken for a boy despite the comic book tees and scraggly lion's mane hair plummeting in front of her face. We have to go to the park for her to be called a boy.

Scottie's garb (at her request) during a visit to the park consisted of her Marty McFly pants and red Flash t-shirt, but flowery pink shoes to complete the outfit. Truly a mystery for some, I suppose. Complicating matters was the fact that Scottie had just received a Green Lantern mask from the neighborhood toy store, and this was the final accessory of her ensemble. Fully decked out, she made her way up the path to a series of benches adjacent to the monkey bars. A much older girl (maybe *seven*) lounged on one of the benches and perked up when I flew Scottie across the path. Scottie asked to be let down, and approached the girl. "I'm Green Lantern and I'm flying!" she purred. The girl was not amused. "You're scaring me," she said, but she was clearly not scared. She was just being a snot. Undeterred, Scottie sat next to her and smiled. Eventually the kid caved to my weewok's charms, and Scottie asked if she wanted to play "da chasing game." The two chased each other until Scottie involved me. "Will you fly me, please, Dada?" I couldn't say no to my little intergalactic peacekeeper, so I lifted her overhead and off we zoomed. The little girl looked to her mother while Scottie and I hurtled toward her. "Uh-uh. You're too big for me to do that," the mom countered. Scottie, ever sensitive, asked if I could fly her new friend. I looked to the mom, who gave me a thumb's up, and I alternated flying the two superheroes (Scottie dubbed her new friend "the Flash," a title that passed over the older girl's head despite her altitude).

Almost an hour after flying, splashing in the malfunctioning water fountain, and swinging on swings, the girls decided to call it quits. The other mom thanked me and told me she was happy my *son* and I could play. Now, this mom was stationary on the bench for quite some time and didn't get a good look at Scottie. But I get it. Her name is Scottie. She likes superheroes. But her splashing and girly glee at swinging might have given away her gender. Or would it have? Why couldn't a little boy wear princess shoes and be equally at home in the superhero world and the princess world?

My little brother Trampas watched and played *My Little Pony*, a habit that I gave him grief about as we were growing up. Yet he was just

166

as comfortable playing Transformers and GI Joe with me. Make whatever inferences you wish, but I even dabbled in *Care Bears* back in the day and I sure thought the opening theme to *Jem and the Holograms* was pretty bitchin'. I think we were lacking in strong female protagonists; *Strawberry Shortcake* just wasn't interesting enough for us. Animals seemed to appeal to both sexes, as boys and girls shared in conversation about the latest episode of Disney's *Gummi Bears* or the aforementioned *Care Bears*. Last year, the kid who played Winthrop in our production of *The Music Man* gifted Scottie his entire collection of *The Littlest Pet Shop* toys. Traditional sensibilities would imply that these are "girl" toys, but looking at them they're incredibly gender neutral. Dogs, cats, lizards, fish, and accessories to build your own pet shop. Does it depend on the animal? Or the way in which it's marketed?

Which brings me to my dislike of McDonald's. Colleen can't stand the place, though we both indulge in a Big Mac every so often. Scottie, like her parents at her age, was unfortunately lured into the Golden Arches with the promise of cheeseburger Happy Meals and the toy surprises. The biggest issue we have with the establishment occurs during ordering. Scottie pipes up sometimes and orders her own Happy Meal, but any customer ordering this meal is asked the following question: "do you want a girl or boy toy?" I understand, I get it, but this perpetuates what I'm talking about. It's certainly easier to place an order, but Scottie has gotten confused. "I'm Scottie, I'm a girl," she'd inform the cashier. I'd stop the cashier, and run through the options. Scottie might prefer the Batman toy to Barbie. Sometimes she does, sometimes she doesn't. And who's to say a little boy doesn't want a Nickelodeon microphone/hairbrush? The distinction between girl and boy toys occasionally leads to inadvertent comedy, such as when McDonald's posted the sign "Sorry- all out of boy toys." One of my pals informed the cashier that when boy toys became available, he'd be sure to stop back for a couple.

***

Sporty Spice

I always thought (and still think) that Sporty Spice was the hottest Spice Girl. Well, okay- Posh Spice was SMOKING HOT, and my college roommates each had different selections. But Sporty always seemed the coolest because she played football, or soccer as I knew the sport back in my Albuquerque Youth Soccer Organization days. Soccer wasn't as sexy a sport as, say, volleyball or swimming. But it wasn't iffy, like the girl's shot put team. Though if Scottie decided shot put was her thing, well… I'd be all for it. Or, you know, 60% enthusiastic about it.

Scottie's first "sport" was weightlifting. As in, she thrilled at attempting to dead lift any object four times her size. She progressed to softball after being gifted a Disney Princess softball by her babysitter.

168

The softball is incorrectly named- the thing is incredible hard, harder than a baseball, and bigger. So... yeah. Scottie would hurl this thing across the house with reckless abandon. We instituted a "roll only" rule, so she'd then precede the roll with a "here we go, here we go bowling!", our cue to prepare for a rocket along the floor. She also has a foam mini-basketball that she enjoys tossing with the warning "here we go, here we go, catch!" Despite this, the sporting bug hasn't fully bit her. I'm trying my best, folks. She has to live up to her Auntie Nay Nay, the free-throw champ of Vista, or good old Tiffany, my racquetball pal.

During the days I frequented racquet clubs with Dad, I used to play cutthroat (3 player) racquetball with my good buddy Van. An incredible athlete, who also happened to have autism, it was incredible to interact with him when playing sports. The confidence he lacked outside of the racquetball court transformed into an assured and wondrous joy when Van blasted the ball for a kill shot. He was funny and warm, and I really dug the time we spent together. After a few months playing against each other, we added another member to our weekly matches. Van's older brother's cousin's former roommate's little sister (or something like that), Tiffany, joined us with a nifty new racquet and a can of balls (I won't pun on that). I was quite adept at racquetball, but Van would consistently work me. Adding Tiffany (who was brilliant at the game) gave him more of a challenge, and gave me even more of an opportunity to get schooled on the court. But Tiffany was witty, jubilant, and the perfect addition to our unique cocktail.

After a match, Van and I would rarely shower since he had to run off to another sport, and I'd sit on the nice couches and sweat while watching TV. Tiffany would retire to the women's locker room and emerge much later with a glorious fanfare (in my mind). She was gorgeous. She dressed well. And her voice was melodious. A trendy lass (as far as the early 90s go), she'd wave goodbye to me on her way to go shopping or whatnot with her girlfriends. Though she was my pal, I was older then than I was when I could think of Shannon only as Vasquez. I *noticed* Tiffany. I noticed her quite a bit.

She was the pride of her father, who admitted to me that she was "the son he never had." I always thought that was funny, despite knowing what he meant. Because Tiffany, to me, was the very definition of "girly."

One of the more intriguing story points in Garth Ennis' legendary comic book series *Preacher* finds a good ol' boy, who longed for a son, saddled with raising a daughter by himself when his wife dies during childbirth. He raises her the same way he'd raise a boy: he teaches her how to shoot a gun and hunt, how to throw a tight spiral, and how to stand up for herself in a fight (no matter the gender of the kid she's fighting). This creates a tough as snot hero, yet the apple of the eponymous Preacher's eye: the delicately named Tulip.

A fictional example, but one that I've seen reflected in many a parent. The reverse holds true, of taking boys who are a bit on the delicate side and forcing them to tackle football dummies or chew tobacco. Certainly Trampas was pushed away from his love of "little girl toons" (Pops) and toward activities or programs that would toughen him up. Thankfully, both he and my younger brother Trever assisted me when rescuing Princess Peach from that brutal bruiser, Bowser (Dad championed alliteration- blame him for its overuse in this book).

***

Games n' girls

On the opposite end of the spectrum from sports, though still considered a very "guy" activity, we have video games. Growing up, I don't remember a single girl who engaged in this activity. Venturing across the street to my pal Joey's place for Nintendo Entertainment System fun always proved difficult. His older sister mocked us to the point of driving me out of the house (the fact that she was incredibly hot didn't help matters).

While Dad supported my habit, Pops took a different stance. Pops (in his Arkansas accent): "I'd almost rather you gamble instead of playing those damn video games. Stick your quarters into a slot machine- at least there's a chance to get something out of it." He didn't understand.

Twirling fruit couldn't hold a candle to slamming the pedal down in *Spy Hunter* or mashing on the buttons of *Track and Field* (I didn't cheat and use the "pencil technique")

In middle school, none of the girls I knew played video games (or admitted to it). During computer class, the girls would occasionally dip into something as benign as *Oregon Trail* on our Apple II computers. But the hardcore gamers would opt for the much more intense *Odell Lake*; made by the same educational game company, players took on the role of a fish. Riveting.

Both sexes eagerly anticipated our eighth grade end-of-year trip: all day play at *The Beach* water park. One of the highlights for me was the two-man beach volleyball tournament, and my partner and I had practiced for months. Terry and I managed to defeat the faculty team, and we had amassed quite an audience during the match. Post-manly activity, I did what all triumphant heroes do: go play video games. Specifically, the *Teenage Mutant Ninja Turtles* arcade game. Four players could play at one time, and some friends and I were determined to beat this game once and for all. We'd never had enough time during lunch or after school (and before rehearsal) to finish the game, and it became financially difficult to continuously pump quarters into the machine. Here at The Beach, riding my volleyball high, I was focused. I was determined. And I also happened to notice the cute redhead in a bikini watching me.

I'd noticed her while engaged in the gladiatorial sand combat. I think I chased a volleyball out of bounds close to where she was standing, and I'll admit I dramatically dove despite the ball being a mile away from any sensible kind of play.

Somewhere around the Turtles' fight with Rocksteady, Ginger and her equally hot friend strolled by. I gave a brief glance and returned to the console. The second time they ambled through the arcade, I definitely perked up. But the rocky General Tragg required a swift ninja dispatch, and Donatello's bo staff was called upon. A couple more passes ensued, and on the final one Ginger brazenly pinched my ass. I wheeled around; I awkwardly smiled/waved (neither landed), nearly fell into the adjacent *Twilight Zone* pinball machine, and hurriedly resumed my combat.

A combination of glee and terror filled me- this girl was into me, right? What the hell was I going to do? Her attraction probably had more to do with my athletic prowess than with my skillful manipulation of Donatello through the droves of foot clan ninjas. But I didn't have the nerve to proceed. Probably an hour or more had passed, and my friends and I finally defeated Shredder and Krang. Congratulations and high fives abounded, but I couldn't stop thinking about Ginger.

I looked around the arcade in vain. She'd gone. I'd missed my

173

opportunity. A voyage down the lazy river's winding current was the only way to forget my courting gaffe.

Ginger's hot friend floated next to me in the lazy river and bluntly asked why I didn't make a move. I craned my neck, but Hot Friend stopped my search. "She's gone, pal." In my usual smooth manner, instead of asking for her number or even her name, I explained that I'd been trying to beat the Ninja Turtles game for months and this looked to be my only shot of doing so. I don't think that endeared me to her. She shrugged and paddled away.

Oddly enough, once I reached high school it was almost cool to hang around the arcade. *Almost* being the operative word. We had an open campus, and my freshman year we explored various hotspots at lunchtime. The mysterious Nunzio's Pizza-to-Go churned out your pizza exactly five minutes from the time you placed your order. It was a bizarre little place with a second story that looked like KITT from *Knight Rider.* Pancho's Taco Shop was another favorite- five meaty tacos for a buck (gotta love 1991). Eventually I discovered the local arcade, which was situated conveniently across the street from our gymnasium. I would save my lunch money and head to MP's Game Room (much better for me than food), named after the good old Montgomery Plaza mini-mall. Incidentally, I'd spend a good part of my high school work career at the M-Plaza movie theatre and shoot many a homemade movie on its rickety escalators.

A few games at MP's were deemed non-geeky, even to the jocks and their girlfriends hanging around. The introduction of *Street Fighter II* created a massive hubbub amongst everyone. At MP's, *SFII* was 2L2Q (too legit to quit). A highly anticipated release, there was always a line of quarters placed along the upper ridge of the machine's title card. This indicated, of course, a place in line to play the game. The original *Street Fighter* was situated in the corner next to the air hockey table, and certainly suffered from lack of use. Another almost-cool game was *G-Loc: Air Battle*, the semi-enclosed F-14 flight combat simulator. You'd sit in this contraption and it would rotate as you opened fire on hostile targets. I enjoyed the experience, and so did the ladies. No, really. Not in the sense of "oh, Lance, you're such a badass at inverted rolly-things and such." But in the sense that they'd actually be seen playing the game.

That period was very brief, as it seemed like my sophomore year brought with it the usual stigma; that video games were only for geeky guys. Any girl who talked about heading to the arcade was deemed an oddball, and even guys would tend to view her as a bit off. It's a shame, for some of the girls with whom I was lucky enough to talk video game shop were quite balanced. Understand, they didn't talk about video games with the fervor I generally injected into my conversations. What a radical shift then to today, as men and women, boys and girls, enjoy games on their smartphones.

Video games have now expanded to become far more than traipsing though Hyrule gathering rupees and slaying rock-spewing octoroks. Consumers slice fruit with their fingers, or send drawings of celebrities to one another in an advanced (though not much more) version of *Pictionary*. The proliferation of personal electronic devices and their apps has redefined what it means to be a "gamer." Both sexes enjoy plugging away at aliens or harvesting zombies on their farm of the undead. They even have discussions about the latest app (I rarely hear them called games). You, yes you, playing solitaire on your ipad. You're a gamer.

While she hasn't gone full tilt into video games, Scottie definitely knows her way around a gaming console. I used to give her the PS2 remote without batteries when she'd request a round of *Katamari Damacy*, but the kid got wise real fast. Now she demands that only one of us play at a time, and she always checks the LED lights on the controller to confirm power.

Katamari is a great game for her- you roll a ball around collecting various items, making your ball grow as big as it can before the timer runs out. Bright flamboyant visuals and an upbeat, catchy soundtrack (remember, the Katamari theme blasted on our car stereo on the way to the hospital for Scottie's birth) have made the game a favorite in our house.

She only plays video games every so often (once a week, if that), and most of the time she wants to watch me play. One game she can't get enough of, though, is *Guitar Hero*. I'm kind of in support of this game, as it's brought quite a few classic tunes to the consciousness of a new generation of rockers. It's thrilling when Scottie tosses me my guitar, and we both crank it up to Guns and Roses' "Sweet Child of Mine" or The Sweet's "Ballroom Blitz." She rocks out a little too hard at times, and the strap gets wound around her neck. Scary rocking.

Guitar Hero, though overstuffed with covers, at least introduces the classics to those unfamiliar with Rush and Van Halen. Van Halen's "You Really Got Me" is one of the only tunes Scottie likes to repeatedly play, having learned it from *Alvin and the Chipmunks: The Squeakel* (I just wrote that; yikes). The movie opens with the Chipmunks jamming to the tune, and Scottie duplicates Alvin's arpeggios on her plastic guitar.

Little geek that she is, she saw the cover to *Star Wars Battlefront* and requested a go against the Empire. But it's a little violent for me to allow it. Likewise with *God of War*. Cool cover, nifty mythology-based game, and incredibly adult. After dismembering monsters the game's hero, Kratos, regains his energy by a full-on nookie session with naked concubines. Per Scottie, "dat is NOT propriate."

More "propriate" titles include *Doctor Mario* (downloaded on our Wii), something her mother enjoyed on the old NES. It's another puzzle game that was "okay" for girls to play and enjoy. Scottie does play *Wii Sports*, and is actually quite good at *WiiFit*'s balance games (particularly head butting soccer balls into the goal). Other kid-friendly offerings lure her in. Playstation's *Flower* receives regular rotation, where you (as the wind) blow petals around a luscious landscape in an effort to bring life to barren fields. Rolling around in *Hamster Ball* is monotonous for me, but the kid asks for it and she gets it. It reminds me of one of those smartphone games that reaches the number one downloaded game on itunes for a day, and then disappears just as rapidly.

I'll give Scottie the last word on video games. The kid, disheartened at her inability to play *God of War*, *Star Wars Battlefront*, or the Earth vs. aliens set in WWII *Resistance: Fall of Man*: "Oh, when I can ride da Hulk ride, den I can play dese games dat are not propriate for me. Remember Daddy- you have to shoot da zombies in da head or dey WILL NOT STOP."

***

What happens when you assume

We make generalizations and stereotypes based on some element of truth. I don't like it, but I get it. However, don't look at that little girl or boy and think you can sum 'em up in a sentence. And for that matter, please don't assume because I'm a man I know nothing about parenting, or laundry, or cooking, or cleaning.

For this I'll always blame the media, but I believe they really are only as powerful as we make them (it). It's not as if the deception comes out of left field; we know celebrities' looks are fabricated, and the celebrities themselves plow through ridiculous diets to meet our society's body image ideals. We know magazine covers are photoshopped and airbrushed, that most of the women in print and on film appear to be manufactured in some plant. We know there's a man behind the curtain, pulling the levers, but **WE** close the curtain ourselves and focus instead on the great and powerful Oz, the ghoul who blusters at us and tells us who we ought to be. Let's take some responsibility and keep the witch's broomstick for ourselves.

9: How to discipline a geek

My philosophy on discipline initially paralleled a training principle I witnessed at Sea World- the LRS technique (least reinforcing stimuli). Bear in mind I wasn't a sea lion trainer, merely an actor who was upstaged by the sea lions and river otters on a daily basis. Some nomenclature is essential for the understanding of this bizarre vocation- the cool flips and shenanigans the animals perform are not "tricks," they are behaviors. And tanks are not tanks- they are "*pools*." The basis for an LRS is this (to the best of my knowledge): when a desired behavior is not achieved, you simply ignore rather than punish, wait until attention is re-established, then reward the correct behavior an animal produces. Definitely the approach we take with Scottie… no. No, we don't. Not remotely. I'll admit I've attempted this technique, but it usually results in crayon drawings on the walls (and the piano). I feel like our discipline game plan, while relatively consistent, evolves daily with Scottie's growth.

Morality is incredibly difficult for me to judge, considering I'll allow my daughter to watch *Raiders* but won't allow her to watch other films seemingly on par in terms of violence and innuendo. It's all subjective. Colleen and I shift frequently- initially *Iron Man* was okay, and now we've tried to curb movies showcasing guns. Some guns (blasters) we've deemed okay, while others are reserved for an older Scottie. There's really no hard and fast rule.

I can't blame my parents. But it was always interesting to me that my conservative Mom and Pops banned many a movie but still let us watch *Pretty Woman* together. For context, I was twelve, Trampas was nine, and Trever was four. In fact, that movie was my first introduction to prostitution (and my little brothers', I'm guessing). I remember wondering how that was okay. *Next of Kin* with Patrick Swayze was fine, even when he was blasting the bad guys. Yet *Back to the Future* was scandalous. It didn't make sense to me. Though I'm sure Scottie will be scratching her head at all the judgment calls Colleen and I have made throughout her lifetime.

***

"Fredo, you're my older brother and I love you. But don't ever take sides with anyone against the Family. Ever."

Lying happened to be THE criminal offense in my father's house. And I unfortunately broke that rule time and time again.

When I was a kid, Mom and Pops had a discipline plan that was fairly consistent. It involved taking a glass paddle (or reasonable facsimile) to our backsides. Dad's discipline was consistent too, though it encapsulated the word he loved to exclaim when I fouled up-

RESTRICTION. Man, being grounded sucked. I loved when Mom and Pops would punish me. A quick spanking, and I was free to do whatever I wanted. Oh, Joey's playing whiffle ball in the street? No problem, buddy- just a couple minutes. I have to have my ass handed to me (in a fashion) and I'll be right out! I worked out the best time to get into mischief, which was away from the house so I'd have to get spanked on location (so to speak). I could deal with a thwack from Mom or Pops in the field better than the carefully fashioned glass paddles at home. They even had a couple different sizes smelted; I pictured some Conan type fellow working at his glass forges to create these instruments of torment. Who sold these things, by the way? Please pardon the digression, but that strikes me as incredibly interesting. Even with the paddles, I became quite proficient at clenching my butt and invoking my acting pedigree by whipping up some tears, then running off to my room. Where I would watch *The Terminator* on TV.

Dad didn't fool around with his punishment, though nary a blow was physically struck. Not only was I banned from playing Nintendo for the night (for staying out past curfew, or another equally awful offense), but I was also assigned extra chores around the house. There were varying tiers of punishment, too. The severity of the crime dictated the length of the restriction, and the option for compound restrictions also existed. No VCR, no comic books, no NES, and I could only read books by Faulkner. Seriously, this was an exact punishment agenda. Every so often I'd receive a temporary reprieve for good behavior though it usually worked in Dad's favor more than mine.

I distinctly remember a time in 1989 when I was acting like a damn snot. Not only was I giving him attitude, I'd also even refused to finish my homework. Still, Dad took pity on me. We were movie pals, after all; best buds whose cinematic experience was enhanced by the camaraderie we shared. I was sulking over some homework and Dad told me to put some shoes on. "You've been pretty good, so I'm lifting restriction for a couple hours." "No, I haven't," I countered. "I've been a jackass." While acknowledging that was true, he asked if I wanted to come with him to see *Lethal Weapon 2*. Of course I did. We went and listened to Danny Glover revoke Joss Ackland's diplomatic immunity, and gasped at the film's conclusion. On our return home, still riding the high of Riggs' and Murtaugh's exploits, I was immediately placed back on restriction. Incidentally, to this day I can't drive behind any vehicle with a roof-mounted surfboard, for fear it will careen through my windshield and into my face at high velocity.

Dad was my best friend, but first and foremost he was a parent. It was apparent he was a parent (that's what he'd call 2/3 of a pun). He made it very clear his job was not to be my best friend, but to raise me as well as a he could so I didn't grow up to be an asshole. I like to think he succeeded, but I'm still working on it.

Mom and Dad regulated grades with the rigidity of Cold War-era Russia. They were both educators, you see. A B+ wasn't good enough for Dad, and Mom pushed me to go for Bs and above. They propelled me into Honors and AP classes. My grades had to be good, and I worked incredibly hard to achieve good marks. Remember, the plan was for me to attend West Point (Dad's influence, of all people- he was Army, Pops was Navy), but I expressed how much I wanted to do theatre. I expect to be equally stern with Scottie when it comes to her education, and already find myself asking for clarity of diction and proper verb tenses.

I went through a period in seventh grade where school was incredibly easy for me, and I breezed through with an A average. Dad acknowledged my accomplishment, and praised it, but noticed a lack of homework. This didn't sit well with him. He started assigning me homework, such as book reports, if a day passed without me bringing schoolwork home. A favorite of his was the assignation of a 100-word report (this was used as punishment as well as homework- I couldn't really tell the difference). He utilized this technique with his students and suited the topic to the transgression. One of his students (and in an instance of "it's a small world after all," one of my college roommates) farted loudly in class. Obviously intentional, Dad assigned him a 200-word report on "Flatulence." Though in all fairness, if Dad did something

184

wrong and a student called him on it, that student could demand a 100-word report of him. And Dad would deliver.

When I hit the ripe old age of four, I'd done something or other that wasn't in keeping with Dad's expectations (no strange occurrence- I was a terror). He wouldn't let me up from the table until I'd written an apology note. I tore off a sheet from a *Big Cheese Pizza* notepad (Dad stockpiled restaurant stationary) and wrote an apology that was truly heartfelt. I folded it into some pseudo-origami, addressed the top/bottom/side/who knows, and handed it to Dad. He patted me on the head. "Thanks Lance. You can get up now." I ran away to play. Dad opened the note and read: "Dear Dad, I'm very sorry about your behavior. Love, Lance."

Scottie can diminish the severity of an offense from time to time, and Colleen and I can't help but applaud the kid's ingenuity. I believe plenty of kids use semantics to defend their case, and Scottie possesses this ability in spades. She hurled a lampshade around in her room and we told her she needed to stop. "You're going to break it, so I need you to cut it out." She continued to disobey and, of course, knocked the lamp over and shattered the shade into a million tiny pieces. I advised her to stand next to the window until I cleaned up the mess, and that even after I'd finished she had to stay there until she acknowledged what she'd done was wrong. The last piece placed into the trashcan, Scottie immediately

185

proclaimed, "I'm apologizing!" Then ZIP! - off she ran onto her next mischievous adventure.

She's also adept at "playing" angry- she crosses her arms and "hmphs" a lot. It's ridiculous, and Colleen and I have difficulty keeping a straight face. Again, depending on the severity Colleen and I won't disguise it- we just laugh. Can't help it. The kid is certainly stubborn and defiant. I was both too, back in my day. But if you're still here with me reading this, you know that.

There are things I did that I still regret to this day, things of which I have a very vivid memory. We'd just returned from my second or third viewing of *The Secret of Nimh* and I was upset with Dad. I think he'd asked me to pick up my plastic frogs. With a snotty air, I told him "You're not my dad. You're my step dad. I'm gonna start calling you step dad." I knew that would hurt him and that's where I went. All this at five, so I was absolutely old enough to know this was horrendous behavior.

In an ironic twist, I was in sixth grade and visiting Mom and Pops in Vegas when Pops and I got into a confrontation in a Costco. He demanded I call him 'Dad' and I said, "look, I mean no disrespect calling you Roy, and we can figure something else out, but I refuse to call you Dad." He and Mom talked and agreed that it was wrong. The endearment 'Pops' came into being, and that's how all of us address him today.

As a freshman, I had my first and only instance of "running

away" after Dad and I had a huge fight (I can't remember about what). I went to Steve's house and played video games. Though I was only gone a few hours, this was serious stuff. Dad was pissed, and I don't blame him one bit. If Scottie did that to me, I'd be furious. I angrily informed him that I didn't want to live with him (another dagger) and he said "fine, go live with your Mom." So for my sophomore year, that's what I did.

Despite acting like a snot more often than not, I had a clear sense of right and wrong from day one. I did my best to maintain my integrity and strove to be "the good guy." Captain America and his very clear sense of black and white appealed to me, and that was what Mom and Dad had instilled in me (independent of each other). This led to an overdeveloped (still) sense of justice and fair play. It was this sense of justice that got me in a bit of trouble when I was ten.

Fifth grade is a maelstrom of rules and rigidity. You're no longer a kid, and you're preparing for a journey into the turbulent waves of middle school (or junior high, whatever you call it). Our teachers maintained unattainable standards when it came to conduct in my ten-year-old estimation. I was a great student (had to be- remember?) and followed rules to the letter. On one occasion I asked my usually reasonable teacher if I could please be excused to the bathroom. She instructed me to hold it until recess. Fair enough. She was talking about macramé, a vital subject to a child's development. I waited a few minutes, and then raised my hand again. An elevated impatience permeated my query to use the john. I was told to wait. Very well. I could wait. Until I couldn't. Since comedy works in threes, I figured asking a third time would be more than an equitable college try, and for a third time I was rebuked. To prove a point, in my righteous fury I leaned back in my seat and got comfortable. Legs apart, I proceeded to let the pee flow through my multi-print jam shorts. Right there in class, slouched in my brown desk/chair contraption. As the pee drizzled onto the floor, my repulsed classmates took cover. Except for my pal, Peter. He understood the point I was making. I'm not making a joke there, for the record. I'm not talking about *my* peter.

Shock is an interesting condition. Equally interesting is the time it takes to leap over the onset of it and transition to anger. This process took about a solid 30 seconds for my teacher. She pointed me toward the door, and directed me to the principal's office. Now, Mom happened to teach first grade at the same school and she was quickly called in to sort out the literal mess. I explained everything and to this day I'm proud of the way Mom handled it. She was furious with the teacher, and *THE* riot act was read. Later, she told me there were better ways of proving my point, but despite the alternatives presented I still felt that I took the best option.

To contrast this awful story, I want to assure you that I did actually learn how to behave. I know I've described how snotty I could be but Mom, Pops, and especially Dad taught me how to be a gentleman. And Mom taught me to give everyone you meet, and everyone with whom you converse, singular focus and respect. In terms of gentlemanly etiquette, Dad presented it as being applicable to both sexes. Hold the door open for someone, regardless of sex. Walk on the street side of the sidewalk when strolling with someone (I asked him about this, and he said that if a car spun out of control, you would bear the brunt of the impact. He told me this when I was six. Is it any wonder I have anxiety when walking with Scottie?). Dad preached "bend over backwards, despite any inconvenience to your personal agenda." Dad's pastor friend told him this was a Christ-like philosophy. Dad just thought it was pretty solid behavior, and reminded his buddy that he was an agnostic Jew (previously an atheist). Religion aside, I equated proper behavior with merely being a good person. I still ask myself: WWCD, What Would Cap Do?

***

Our children are reflections of us. Like in Scott Pilgrim vs. the World when Scott faces Mirror Scott but instead of fighting, the two decide to hang out and drink coffee.

Scottie's anxiety inevitably displays itself when discipline becomes an issue. But it quickly evolves (or devolves) into a nasty anger.

189

I know it's normal. I know it's natural. But when she's uber-upset and spews out "you are trouble! You get out! I don't want you!" it's hard to take it in stride. For massive freak-outs, we ran through the gamut of disciplinary action. Time-outs, stern warnings, restrictions, removal of toys and television privileges, and even the good old LRS: each of these only served to escalate the situation. We resorted to holding her tightly, a technique Colleen's Mom utilized when my dear wife was a wee lass. This worked fairly well for us- until it didn't. She started getting more worked up, and even bit us a few times.

We finally found a solution that has worked well; or rather Scottie has become old enough to understand (to a degree) her transgression. That said, I'm fully expecting us to have to alter our approach as Scottie changes her viewpoint on the whole discipline thing.

Getting her to acknowledge the close of an activity or having to leave a place proves incredibly difficult. So we set the alarm on our iphones to a festive marimba, or let her pick which music will play when it's time to go. We'll also set this alarm for bedtime, or toy pickup, or… anything else. This works, but the kid's intuitive nature plays to her advantage quite often.

These smarts manifest when she requests her bobo fett. She'll be sitting quietly, reading or writing the next great American novel, when she'll suddenly blast "Hey guys!" to get our attention. Three fake sneezes follow; I'm not kidding, the child knows the comedy law of threes, then she sniffles, "I'm so sick. I need my bobo fett to make me feel better."

With a growing vocabulary, it's certainly been easier to understand when and why she's upset. Though she'll now have a tantrum every so often, she'll inform us "whoa, now, I need to have some space, please." She most often retreats to the laundry room. There in the piles of socks and comic book tees she re-centers herself and quells her inner tempest.

For the longest time, eye contact was a tricky avenue for our weewok. Even when not in trouble, her focus was all over the place. We recently had a breakthrough in this arena; it occurred during a visit to Disneyland and a kingly feast at Medieval Times. To hawk their upcoming Pixar film *Brave*, Disneyland had marked off a large area outside of *It's a Small World* dedicated entirely to the Scottish-set movie. The highlight was getting to meet the film's hero, curly-headed Merida. Not only did Scottie respond to Merida's questions, but she even turned back to us at many points and asked us if she could participate in the archery range behind the princess. For the rest of the day, any inquiry was meet with full eye contact.

And at Medieval Times, she had but to take one glance at our knight (she thought he looked like Thor) before she was smitten. We met him after the show and, as with Merida, she looked into his near-

Asgardian eyes for the entire conversation. He told her to be strong and do the right thing (something I try to reiterate constantly). She curtsied to him, and promised to "be da good guy all da time."

Scottie has blossomed in her sense of heroism and fair play. Colleen came home to find Scottie, Bit (her sitter), and Josh (her sitter's boyfriend) engaged in a massive superhero battle. Bit blocked Josh's Hulk fists with her Captain America shield, while Scottie flew around the couch with Thor's hammer. All three turned to face Colleen, and Scottie instructed them to "go get Mama now!" Bit and Josh squared off, but Scottie's heroic instinct kicked in. In the blink of an eye (or a few blinks-she can only move so fast when accoutered with a giant hammer and blanket/cape), she soared down from her perch. Twirling mighty Mjolnir over her head, she intercepted the wayward heroes, placing her body between them and her celestial mother. "You can not come here, bad guys! I will protect you, Mama."

This sudden awareness manifests at the end of a tantrum, too. She knows she's in the wrong, she knows when she's out of line. After a particularly nasty tirade, and a moment of consideration, the only thing Scottie could offer was, "I'm sorry, Mama. I'm just... I'm fwawed, Mama. I'm fwawed."

***

One of the best days, yet the worst day ever (to date)

Truly that was a benchmark day of parenthood. Feeling like nothing, even a *Deep Impact*-sized tidal wave, could come between you and your daughter. Then the asteroid hits and like Tea Leoni in that better-than-*Armageddon* film, your world is gone.

The day began happier than most preschool days. Getting Scottie to rise by 7 proves to be difficult when you actually need her to awaken. However, on this day she rose with a smile and an "oh hi Dada! It's so nice to see you here." Joyous. She slipped into her brown corduroy jeans with nary a complaint, which is completely out of the ordinary. She agreed to a face wash, and even brushed her teeth herself.

She wanted to bring her *Cat in the Hat* book to school, a practice I encouraged. We laughed and started in on our usual pre-preschool car routine. She ate some yogurt and toast, and requested the *Tron: Legacy* soundtrack. Smiling, I interrupted Daft Punk and asked what she wanted to do at school. "I tell dem about Disneyland, Dada." She also mentioned her book again, and wanted to talk about the National Theatre's production of *The Cat in the Hat* that we had streamed over Netflix. She reiterated how much she loved me, took a final swig of juice, and readied herself for school.

We parked and jogged our way to the front doors (again, a ritual for us). She greeted Karen at the front desk and made her way to her classroom, the Seedlings. We passed the Ducklings and, though this area is separate from her classroom, she shouted tidings of "it's a wonderful day, everybody". She led me by the bottom of my shirt to where a few of the Seedlings were painting. Definitely one of her favorite activities, she once gave me a painting that I put into my special Starbucks cup's liner. I thanked her for it, and asked what it was. "Paint, dada. Dat's paint."

Kneeling down to her, I bade her adieu and she planted a big kiss on me. She waved and ran off to join her classmates. Riding high, I strode out of that preschool, into Colleen's blue Honda Civic, and floored it (well, I went 15 mph; the school is on USD's campus, after all).

My time at home was relatively uneventful; a handful of bills and some babysitting booking. Thrilled to be getting work done, I couldn't wait to pick her up.

As I rounded the corner toward her classroom, the sound of her giggles broke me into a run toward her. Held aloft by Teacher Michelle's daughter Amanda (whom she adores), she extended both arms toward me and laughed "Dada's here! Yay!" She dropped to the ground, quite gracefully I might add, and sprinted toward me. Biggest hug ever.

"Bye everybody! I have to go get my bobo fett and drink juice on da couch and watch George." I had promised her she could watch *Curious George* after school and before her nap, provided she eat all/most of her lunch. I figured the usual cheeseburger on Milton's would suffice. I figured correctly. She devoured it, watched some George, and agreed to take her nap when I told her it was time (when the alarm went off, naturally).

Armed with a bobo fett and her brown elephant blanket (her favorite in a collection that includes a monkey, paisley flowers, and a fluffy pink one from Auntie Mar), she sidled into bed asking only for a story- *Grandpa Green*, that tale of a horticulturist whose plant sculptures remind him of a life well-lived. The story concluded, Scottie smiled, hugged and kissed me, and rolled over. "Good guys n' gals" and "I love you, thwip" completed, I softly closed the door.

More uneventful, but important, househusband time commenced. I think I washed the dishes and separated clothes for the laundry. Scottie slumbered soundly. One load went into the laundry, then another. Chores completed, I lounged on the couch and finished watching *Drive*, a kick-ass film that isn't actiony enough for some, and too violent for others. It, like baby bear's chair for Goldilocks, was just right for me.

Occasionally, Scottie will wake up from her nap in a deep (and vocal) funk. Thumps occur, and werewolf growls emanate from her room. Comfort in these cases consists of letting her scream in my face, tears loping down her cheek. But not that day. That day, she creaked open her door and called down. "Dada? Dada, I'm awake. Are you okay?" Knock, knock, on the gate upstairs. I moved up and lifted her over the barrier. She showed me her blanket and bobo fett, a question in her glance. "You need to leave those in your bed, please, honey." She acquiesced, and even seemed to quickly accomplish the task. A reward was in order.

Scottie developed a love of Studio Ghibli without me. That's the anime studio behind critical hits *Princess Mononoke* and *Spirited Away*, though my favorites have been *Kiki's Delivery Service* and *My Neighbor Totoro* (Ghibli geeks will notice Totoro as one of Bonnie's toys in *Toy Story 3*). According to Colleen and various sitters, she happened upon *Howl's Moving Castle* through Netflix streaming and has become captivated by Hayao Miyazaki's worlds. So for her reward she begged to see the new Ghibli/Disney joint *The Secret World of Arrietty*, based on the book *The Borrowers*.

Trailers make or break films, but I think the Arrietty character could have been shown watching stucco dry and Scottie would have wanted to see it based on the preview. Since lunch was out of the way, I allowed her to have a popcorn and even sprung for the medium (the kid can pack away a medium by herself, but we normally get a small just for her). Calm but content, we found our way to "teeter 2" which Scottie easily identified. Settling in, we waited for the previews.

Watching previews with Scottie can be exhilarating. She treats each one like a mini movie, and reacts accordingly. Hollywood, take note: screen your trailers for toddlers and learn how to cut a proper preview. *The Lorax* was mixed with a blend of subtle comedy and broad slapstick that Scottie thoroughly enjoyed. She even tugged my elbow, laughing, "silly Dr. Seuss" and "he wants to save da trees, Dada." I wasn't as impressed, but I'm sure we'll see it. Disney Nature's *Chimpanzee* commanded both of our attentions, and *ParaNorman*'s use of the Donovan groove "Season of the Witch" secured the film a spot on both of our must-see lists. After the previews, *Arrietty* began in earnest. Earnestly slow-paced. As explained earlier, Scottie is a near-perfect audience member and certainly in the top percentile when it comes to theatre etiquette. But it's a very slow film.

While not one of my favorite Ghiblis, *Arrietty* was poignant and simply beautiful. It delved into themes like divorce and the fear of dying quite gracefully- though Scottie and I didn't discuss either of those items. Colleen and I like to discuss with Scottie any media we encounter together. I decided not to broach these subjects (we've talked about death before) unless Scottie asked.

A few moments of shifting in her seat notwithstanding, she did wonderfully. And she seemed to enjoy the film. She relished Arrietty's unique style, and tried to emulate the clip the little Borrower used to keep her hair up. Scottie, mimicking but also considering, held up a long strand of her hair on either side to get "the look". And then she continued to watch the film, hands held high with hair (but out of anyone's eye line).

We left the theatre in a mutual sense of elation; she for having gone to a fun movie and devouring a tub of popcorn, and me for this incredible day. All too quickly, the Battle of Hogwarts descended upon us.

Antsy after a ninety-minute movie, she naturally wanted to run around like a whacko. Totally cool. She ran down the hall, stopping only to examine the movie posters for *Men in Black III* (why, child?) and predictably, *The Avengers*. I ran after her for a bit until she reversed course, making for the lobby and the video games. Again, I was fine with all this, and knew that she'd get a little bit of energy out, and then we'd go to the park, perhaps. After the park we might have dinner, a bath, a story or three, and bedtime. Our usual, but flexible, routine.

I informed Scottie it was time to go home, but I needed to change her bulging diaper first. She refused. I asked again, firmly. Then I stopped asking, and told her we were going to the bathroom to change her diaper. She emphatically told me to "go away", something Colleen and I have discouraged since she began it a few months ago. I told her it was unacceptable to talk to me that way, and she screamed. The girl has lungs, and she let everyone in the theatre know that she was unhappy.

"STOP IT! I DON'T WANT TO GO WITH YOU! LEAVE ME

ALONE! STOP IT, DON'T TOUCH ME, STOP IT GO AWAY!!!!" I let

her get it out, then picked her up and made an effort to haul her to the

bathroom. She hit me as hard as she could in the face, an action that

earns an immediate timeout. Forgoing the diaper change (we were 5

minutes from home) I opted to deal with this at our place. She hit,

kicked, and screamed all the way to the car and when I attempted to strap

her into her car seat, she took both hands and shoved my face. Hard.

She's gotten out of her car seat a couple times before, though

thankfully not completely out. We explained the safety issues involved,

and she seems to understand. "I could get hurt, and den I'd have to go to

da doctor." As we drove up the hill to our apartment, Scottie (who hadn't

stopped screaming and thrashing) ripped her arms out of the restraints

and worked at the buckle holding her lower half in the seat. Had we been

at a stop, or even somewhere to pull over, I could have taken her out and

talked her down (or so I thought). But we were headed up a long hill,

with traffic behind us. I made the unfortunate decision to wear a Bengals

hoodie, though not unfortunate because of the team (I know, I know).

The hood provided an excellent handhold for Scottie's outstretched arms.

At this point I stress again that we were IN MOTION, and she

had never done that before (and hasn't since). The weewok is strong, and

this yanked me back. Thankfully, a light was fast approaching, and with

my right hand I was able to disengage and at least hold her back in her seat. "Carmen Scotland Smith, sit back in that seat and don't EVER do that again." I was angry, and louder than I ever like to be. But her vocal onslaught continued, and we pulled up to the light.

I whipped around and cinched her back into the car seat, amidst protestations and blows to my body. Red light. Thank Zeus. The screaming and body convulsing intensified, and I did the only sensible thing I could think of. "If you want your bobo fett, you've got to calm down, Scottie." Screams. Chaos. And a decision. Bye-bye, bobo fett.

I held it up, told her to bid it adieu, rolled down the window, and chucked it out onto the street. I harbored no delusions that this would calm her down in the short-term; my hope was that, in the long term, it would both make her realize that her behavior can sometimes lead to less-than-desirable results, and that we'd be able to wean her off the pacifier. This makes it sound as if I made a careful, considered decision. No, no. Far from it. I was beyond furious, and I was human (though no longer, with the invention of Cyberdyne industries).

The barrage of high-decibel insults didn't cease, though there was a definite sense of both "I can't believe he did that" and "what am I gonna do now?" I felt horrible, but stubbornly defended my decision. Scottie moaned "why, Dada? Why would you do dat? You don't throw things, Dada! You don't throw!" I responded to each question, but my responses went unheard. Scottie's screams had turned into weeping blats.

200

It was tragic. When I carried her out of her car seat, she lowered her head onto my shoulder. I thought the battle had ended. It would begin anew once inside.

I set her down as I fumbled with the keys. Her fists clenched, tears cascading down her cheeks, she slowly shuffled into the living room. I offered her milk, juice, a pony- anything at all, but she remained silent.

It was time for a diaper change, then a bath, then bedtime. She would have none of it. "I WILL NOT CHANGE MY DIAPER. NO DIAPER. NOT EVER." More insults, something like "Leave now, Dada! I don't want you. You are NOT my daddy." Heartbreaking, and not all that dissimilar to when I called my own father "stepdad" to hurt his feelings.

Scottie (and all children, I believe) has the ability to become completely and effectively immovable. Her diaper was bulging, but thankfully hadn't begun to dump its contents. I hefted her stiff body in the air and brought her back into the living room. The diaper change forced me to use Leg Restraint 101 that you learn when they're babies. With one hand and knee, you wedge one of her legs down, while the other hand attempts to wipe and put on the new diaper. Warm up your neck, as you'll have to dodge the errant blows to the face.

Mercifully, Colleen came home shortly after the diaper change, and was able to add a level head to the conflict. Scottie glared at me as if we'd die enemies. That's extreme, but in all sincerity I felt as if she truly hated me. And that's perhaps the worst I've ever felt. Nothing I could do or say brought reason to her demeanor. She was three. I knew that. Still, I'd never seen her that way before.

More waterworks, none feigned, and she explained to Colleen what I had done. "Den he threw it out da window. Dada threw it. I cried, because he- no throwing Dada! I tell him, no throwing!" I tried to explain, but Colleen tossed me "the look", indicating I should retire to the living room while she took Scottie upstairs.

Sadly, I grabbed my little weewok's flower blanket off the couch and folded it up. I wanted to be useful, to some degree. Upstairs, the calming process had begun. Downstairs, I was still lost.

The reconciliation was truncated and despite me reiterating "Scottie, honey, I love you very much" she was adamantly angry. Out of the corner of her mouth, Colleen whispered "apologize" and I complied. Scottie recommended I not throw her bobo fett out the window, or anywhere, in the future. In my stubbornness, I agreed that the action of throwing it was wrong, but not the need for the action. Too damn stubborn, this fella.

I kissed Scottie and she gave me a feeble hug. That was all it took to break me again, and I slinked off to bed. Colleen came in moments later, much to my utter astonishment. No way Scottie went down so quickly, I thought. But nary a peep emanated from the weewok's room.

"What did you do?" I asked, truly curious even in my shame. Colleen smiled and patted my noggin. "You may need to go get a Hello Kitty ring pop." She told Scottie that the Bobo Fairy would scoop up that pacifier that was lying on the blackened road, and would deliver it to some child that needed it. In return, the Bobo Fairy would be leaving a special treat under Scottie's pillow for giving up her bobo fett (albeit against her wishes). In the words of Threepio, "thank the maker" for Colleen.

No more talk; just a kiss, and I trudged out to the 7-11 for a pink (her favorite) Hello Kitty ring pop. I guess it was fortunate for me that they were in stock as they've been known to run out, and that heaps copious amounts of grief on our child and, consequently, our family.

The following morning, Scottie awoke and was as surprised as we were to find she made it through the whole night without her bobo fett. We praised her profusely, and I think I even hefted her overhead with pride. She beamed, and I told her to look under her pillow. Lo and behold, the prize- Scottie tore into it with a voracious intensity not often on display. The Bobo Fairy had come, sure enough. I apologized again, and Scottie said she too was sorry for "not listening and screaming and crying and kicking and hitting and saying bad things."

The worst day was over. A new day with my wife and daughter had begun.

10: Living the Example- Our responsibility as stewards of the next generation

Okay- so there's an entire generation of geeks running amok, spreading their doctrine of awesomeness throughout the land. I've touched on the beliefs and practices I use in raising my little weewok. But what can I do *for myself* to be the best person I can be? I mentioned trying to live by Captain America's unattainable standards, and while unattainable, I think about it every day. I find that my successes are matched by my screw-ups, but every opportunity for growth gives me hope (well, most opportunities).

As a fifteen-year-old geek, I found joy in mowing lawns. Being outside and trimming the yard, even in Las Vegas' blistering 100+ heat, proved idyllic for me. My first real job (no work permit) was assisting a landscaper in sweltering Las Vegas. I felt like a normal kid when cutting grass. When Dad died that first week of college, I wanted to find a sanctuary of my own. I was absolutely numb, and needed not to be around a place I'd known with him. So the hunt began for a house to rent, the major criteria being that it have a lawn.

Describing this desire to my best friend Ron (who I met when we were both five- he was throwing a football to himself and I asked if he wanted someone with whom to play catch), I touted this as simply wanting to feel normal: especially after Dad's death, the instability of the acting profession I was pursuing permeated my consciousness.

Eventually finding a house with five other guys, when divvying up household chores I jumped at mowing the lawn (I later had to do more than that). Now I don't have a lawn, but I have a family. And chores. Many, many chores. But a desire for family was, I think, at the core of what I considered "normal." Yet how to keep and prove worthy of the gift of family? I had no idea, and I'm still slugging my way through it, like Thor proving his worth to Odin.

One way is through fidelity. It seems Colleen and I are at an age (she's younger than me) where a large number of our friends are going through divorces, many as a result of infidelity. I comprehend it, to a degree. Since we desire connection and our reality is defined by our connections, when the connection in your own marriage falters it's easy to be lured into even the tiniest spark elsewhere. When it comes to women I find many of them attractive intellectually and physically (and both), but again it's a matter of *choice*. I choose to love my wife and my family, as they choose to love me.

As an actor, I recognize the lure of infidelity. Regardless of whether you're intimate physically in a scene with another actor, or you conduct an emotional affair (your character, rather). Again, it's about choice. I just shot an industrial where I played a schmucky guy who is seduced by a woman at a nightclub. Once in a blue moon I'll play a romantic lead, but my usual trade is that of the character actor or the villain. During this shoot, I had to make out with my costar. I ran it past Colleen, who wasn't thrilled, to be sure, but appreciated that I made sure it wasn't crossing any line. It's all about your morality barometer.

There is definitely a line I won't cross as an actor. Not just for my wife, but for the sake of my child. My ex-wife was called upon to simulate some explicit stuff in Brad Fraser's *Unidentified Human Remains and the True Nature of Love*. I remember her bringing me the script to see if I was okay with it. I wanted to be supportive, but did express how uncomfortable I was with the whole thing. I asked her not to do it, and she did it anyway. Which again, as an artist, I understand. But as a husband, I was a wreck.

In the immortal *Clerks*, Silent Bob (Kevin Smith) finally speaks his wisdom aloud when Dante wants to leave his loving girlfriend to get back together with an ex: "You know, there's a million fine women in the world, but not all of them bring you lasagna at work- most of them just cheat on you." There's a bit of truth in this, in that a choice has to be made. That choice is key. I don't believe in the whole "love at first sight" axiom; there is a multitude of attractive, intelligent, funny people in this world. How could there be only one person for you? Mathematically, the odds are against it. Please don't misjudge me- I'm romantic, but in an unconventional sense.

Romance is when Colleen, though groggy, rubs my bald head for twenty seconds before falling asleep. It's sitting on the couch together talking through a trip to the apple pie shops in Julian, a chill mountain town near San Diego. It's putting up a wish board encapsulating goals simple (finish the book that you, the reader, have in your hands), complex (for Colleen, get her PhD), and the simply complex (be good parents). When working at the theatre, we do our best to make dates out of dinner breaks. A nearby park provides an avenue of escape. Trips to this park to have some wine and homemade sandwiches give us time to reconnect, and we make this a priority as often as possible. The practical un-romanticness of it is exactly what makes it romantic. And we love each other. In the words of Stan Lee, "nuff said."

***

Let Wapner Judge

Feeling confident about family is an incredible feeling. But it's difficult, for anyone I suppose, not to judge others by your own experience. I'm guilty as hell about this. Too often I see things in black and white, and shift to grey only when it's convenient for me. Again, Cap sees the world this way (at least he did until the whole *Civil War* storyline Marvel instituted a few years back). Geeks are, by nature, incredibly judgmental. We build our worlds out of passion and we cling to those worlds with unyielding fortitude. Heaven forbid our world should come tumbling down with the introduction of a foreign element, so we protect our domain with fervor.

The Internet and social media fuel this fury, giving us undreamed of access to our favorite sports, authors, eccentricities, and obsessions. I still maintain that the Internet is a useful tool. I think Facebook, like anything else, has the potential to do tremendous damage. But I enjoy re-connecting with friends long gone. The callous attitude of "I've kept in touch with everyone from high school I cared to" is weak. The other incredible thing about the Internet is the ability to remedy any gaps in knowledge instantly, and to compare multiple sources. Yet with this knowledge must come temperance. Leaked photographs of the new Superman costume caused snap judgments from fanboys like "this movie will obviously be atrocious since he's not wearing his red Underoos."

It's human nature to judge and geeks possess this trait, albeit heightened to the nth degree. Geeks share this characteristic with preschoolers' parents. In this particular case I'm not referring to myself (though it certainly applies), but to the father of Scottie's classmate.

Preschool arrival time is usually a crapshoot. Scottie's mood could change on a dime and after waking up and devouring breakfast, she could decide to strip naked and climb her old crib (it's happened).

Each time we get into the car with a minimum of fuss I feel as if Sisyphus has finally pushed the rock up the hill. It's usually smooth sailing from here on out. We park, and Scottie immediately goes into "how can I stall going to school" mode. After a brief run through the purple flowers outside, she may resolve that it's more fun to book it on the sidewalk than to engage in her studies. Then there's the lure of the lobby. Not only can visit time happen with Ms. Karen and Jacquie (the head of the school), but there's a pad of paper and some colored pencils for her to write her name and rival Seurat's neo-impressionist masterpieces.

For a time, until his daughter graduated to kindergarten, I'd run into a Dad on his way into the opposite classroom. More often than not, he'd cast a disparaging glance our direction as Scottie and I doodled fantastic worlds and words on the provided pad. This particular day, I had to take Scottie out of school early for a trip up north to visit cousin AJ. Normally this would pose no problem. It'd be a simple "bye and have a good nap everybody!" Not so this time. She was entrenched in her "castle"- a set of stairs leading to a loft adorned with drapes and princess trappings. Grace was leading story time for the majority of the children, and our normal M.O. is to say, "Excuse us" or "Sorry to interrupt story time." The kid wasn't leaving without a fight this time. I had to whisk her away quickly, and literally kicking and screaming (her more than me...)

we passed through the foyer. We made it to the lobby when DD (disparaging Dad) came out with his little girl. He chuckled and had to comment. "Tough time leaving, huh?" I answered with the only thing I could- "yep."

He continued: "Yeah, I know enough not to pull my daughter out of class during story time." I smiled, politely. This meant, "Yep, I got it, EXPLETIVE EXPLETIVE." Apparently he took this as an invitation to expound. "You know, story time is important for them, socially. They..." I tuned out. Scottie was screaming and I decided retreat the better part of valor. I could feel his judgment following us out the door, into the car, and though she calmed down instantly, onto Interstate 8. I couldn't hold a grudge, though. I simply re-evaluated my own behavior and found it to be lacking in compassion at times. That story will remind me of compassion, and I don't think I'll ever forget it (the story itself; I'm sure my behavior will falter more than once in the near future).

Recently at Disneyland I saw a kid that looked like he was probably six or so, perhaps older, walking with a bobo fett (pacifiers will always be bobo fetts to me) and it reminded me how prone we are to judgment. In the pre-baby past, I would have gone on about how he's too old to suck on a pacifier, and when I have kids I'll never let her do that. However, I don't want her to be six and still have need of a bobo fett, and I don't think she will, but I believe I've become less judgmental about parenting now that my weewok is around. My first thought this time was- what's going on? Are they having a bad day? Did they need to placate him? Does he need it? My focus was on what could have possibly happened as opposed to snapping to judgment. It reminded me how prone we are to judgment, myself included.

***

Dear Scottie: Please tell your story, and do the right thing. Always.

When your Mom had the idea to set up an email address for you, I leapt at the opportunity to send you correspondence throughout the years. It'll still be some time before you access it (or maybe not, adept as you are at manipulating technology), but you'll see your progression from birth till present through the eyes of your parents. You'll also have this book, so in keeping with the theme of this final chapter I'm going to tell you everything I feel for you, weewok. I know you're already tired of my lectures, but perhaps this will flow a little less clinically.

Some of my earliest memories are from when I was about your age. I remember sitting on a pony at church with your Uncle Trampas. I was probably four, holding a one-year-old on my lap. On a pony. I remember the tunes Dad's musical car horn played. You could type in any number from 1-99 and the horn would play the theme from *Cheers* or the opening fanfare from *Star Wars*. Dad (your Papa Smith) invented the song that you and I sing today. "We're going to the zoo, we're going to the zoo! Lancey and Daddy and little Nicky too" was the gist of it. I love the enthusiasm you present when you sing "Scottie and Daddy and…" and you start inserting people and things. "Scottie and Daddy and da car, and da light on da roof of da car."

I love that you ask Mom to paint your "pony nails." I love that you say "deal" and extend your hand when offering only one option. I love that when you offer multiple options they're always in your favor ("so I can go to bed now and eat ice cream, or I can stay on da couch and eat ice cream while I watch da *Fresh Beat Band*"). I love the way you sing "Beyond the Sea" like Will Ferrell's impression of Robert Goulet. I love that you've noticed the way you speak, and consciously catch yourself when you say "da" instead of "the."

I'm sad that you never got to meet your Papa Smith or your Papa Kollar (I didn't get to meet him, either). But know that by the time you read this Mom and I will have filled your head with tales of your two Grandpas long gone. You've already asked a few questions about each of them. I love that you ask even more questions every time I give you an answer. Seriously- I do.

Continue to ask questions as you grow, kid of mine. You've lately taken to ask, "Why is that?", a variation on my own "how come?" when I was your age. You do it because you are truly curious, and like cutting the head off a hydra causes two more to spring forth, each answer to a question reveals multiple threads of new inquiries. I used to drag out my encyclopedias and follow each new thread. By the time you read this book, you'll probably be sick of my "extend your dendrites" mantra. You now have the Internet and the information you crave is but a click away. Use it. Revel in it. Let your curiosity run rampant. Always ask "why?" my love, and never lose your sense of wonder.

Love, Dad

***

Our stories can save the world

Now that's an oversimplification, sure, but it's what I believe. During my morning commute, NPR was already dialed in on the radio so I gave it a listen. Right off the bat was a story about rockets fired on Israel. Schools continued to be closed, the BBC world reporter mentioned. 1.7 million people live on the Gaza strip, an area that is only twenty-five miles long and between three and eight miles wide. In this relatively small area, the reporter divulged, among the casualties in the night were a young boy and an old man. Israel had retaliated, sending rockets that were targeting Hamas leaders. This story segued into another about so-called "kill squads" of American soldiers killing Afghans for fun. It started my speculation on the notion of storytelling. Where can our stories merge where it matters? How can a global story congeal to overcome this conflict and make us work together for the betterment of the planet? Ay, there's the rub.

Dad was an incredible storyteller. Yet he acknowledged that our stories would be naught but for myths and religions. He told me that these ancient stories sprang from the first storytellers; someone had to witness these events. He mentioned a fellow named Joseph Campbell and his studies into world storytelling. I was told to follow Ariadne's thread through the labyrinth; Dad was clear that I wouldn't emerge from the maze unscathed, but I'd have a lifetime of experience. While it's impossible to follow all the threads of life, I'm happy with the tenuous grip I have on this particular one.

I subscribe to Joseph Campbell's ideas on what he terms the "Monomyth"- where myth isn't a synonym for 'false', but rather implies a universal truth, an all-encompassing story we share simply by living and filling that life with adventures. Even seemingly mundane activities imbue the monomyth with stories to which we can relate. Last year, the nonprofit group Invisible Children launched their KONY 2012 campaign, and told a story through moving images that educated and issued a call to action. Filmmaker Andrew Stanton (*Finding Nemo*, *Wall-E*, and the not as bad you've heard but should've been way better *John Carter*) participated in the acclaimed TED Talk series and spoke on story: he said, "Make us care" about your story, and that's where the truth lies (regardless of whether the story contains little actual fact). When a political candidate gives a speech, it oftentimes incorporates a personal story, a story that reflects on all Americans/citizens of this world to make us care. Certain localized stories that don't apply to us can be rewritten universally, or the candidate can tell the story so well that we graft it onto our own situation.

The purpose of telling a story is to connect with at least one other person: storytelling, by definition is a communal experience. Everybody has their own personal story, and different things are important to different people. It's finding where the overlap/commonalities are in our individual stories that is the real trick of it all. What's my life story? It's the need to live, to protect my family and myself, the need to provide, the need to make this world a better place. I'm sure you can relate.

There's a responsibility in story, another imperative Andrew Stanton states. In telling a story you're essentially making a contract, a promise, to the audience that this story will be worth their time. And that's absolutely right. Elevating your story to such a level that it is important to you will make your audience invest in it as well.

Sadly conflict will always exist. Conflict is the essence of drama, the essence of a good tale. Without conflict you don't have a solid story. But it's overcoming that adversity that gives us the crux of a well-told

story. Lamb's Players' mission statement is "to tell good stories well."
We love stories that showcase triumph in the face of adversity. When
two characters overlap stories they then find it easier to fend off a
common threat. There has to be one element of our own storylines that
can link up with another's storyline, and accomplishing this feat creates
an extension of your own path.

What is your storyline? Joseph Campbell describes it so well in
The Hero with a Thousand Faces. Your storyline, your path isn't as if
you're walking through a tunnel; rather, it's a dirt path in the woods, little
splinters, little trails, animals crossing in and out, branches falling down.
At several points, every so often, the path splits into one or more other
ways to pass. This is a nexus point- you have to make a choice. I used to
wonder as a kid if there were some alternate reality me who chose not to
knock over that lamp. And later, in college, I speculated as to the other
me who decided to go to West Point. One of the biggest choices of my
life was deciding whether to move to San Diego and work at Sea World,
or to stay in LA and work at Fox Sports as the assistant CFO. I chose Sea
World.

Digby told his playwriting students that the basis for every good
story is the answer to the question "why is today different than any other
day?" How extraordinary it would be to treat every day with this tenet!

That's one thing Scottie's just beginning to understand. I love

217

when she tells us her own Scottie the Saucer Girl story, incorporating Colleen and me into her world. Most of us aspire to be more than what we are. Stories help us do just that. Scottie absolutely strives to make each day different than the day before. I wish I could do that, at least with some consistency.

Story can connect the world and we all have the ability/responsibility to participate. Keep open to everybody's stories, and tell them yours.

***

Legacy/Mortality

Earlier I asked 'why is it so important to me to school my daughter in things that may not be immediately relevant to her life?' Well, they *are* relevant. She'll pick and choose what she needs, consciously, but she'll have a piece of all of it simmering in her subconscious. Ultimately, I'd like to leave a legacy of story to the weewok. I want her to be the hero. She tries to be, even now.

Colleen and I are at an age where our contemporaries are breaking through to universally accepted success in their given fields. This makes me aware not only of what kind of world Scottie and her generation will inherit, but what my personal responsibility is to her future landscape.

I have to ask myself Kazim's question from *Last Crusade:* "Do you seek the Grail for His glory? Or for yours?" Though my answer is complex, I have to side with Indy: I'm just looking for my father, in a way. And looking for the ways he taught me to behave.

The idea of a hero is certainly tagged as a product of geekdom but as I've expressed, its roots in history abound. The way we deal with death says a great deal about our heroism. We could give up, and some do, for a time. But I've witnessed countless folks recover and build on such a crushing loss. At the age of eight I lost one of my soccer buddies. Brad lived around the corner from me, and we'd head off to soccer practice together. He and I, and the other kids in close proximity, would do magic shows together for the neighborhood. We'd take a bug, wrap it in cellophane and put it in our mouths. Brad died when a kid in the building next door was taking shots with a gun at the lock on his gate. Brad was on the other side, and the bullet hit him. One moment my fellow magician was there, the next he was hurtling into the unknown. I wasn't there, but the repercussions slammed into me. My friends rallied around each other and though we didn't fully understand the loss, we remembered Brad and his virtues every day.

Some years later I witnessed an incredibly heroic act performed by Mom and Pops. Dragging our Prowler trailer around the hills on return from vacation (probably the one where Pops begrudgingly took us to see *Batman Returns*) we happened upon a surveyor lying in the middle of the road. He'd been hit by a car, and the car didn't stick around. After calling 911 and flagging down another vehicle for assistance, Mom ran into the trailer and got some blankets for the guy while Pops cleaned him up. I remember Mom and Pops telling us to stay in the truck. They asked for my help in taking care of Trampas and Trever. I recall looking back through the window while Mom and Pops stayed with this man, giving him water and company until he died. After finishing with the authorities, they returned to the truck in silence. They held hands, asked if we were okay, and drove off.

I'd moved back from Vegas to Albuquerque at the end of my sophomore year when Dad was diagnosed with cancer (thankfully Dad allowed this snot bucket back). Despite this, I refused to acknowledge his mortality. I didn't think for a second that he wouldn't be able to beat it. Life continued apace. My senior year, I joined the Track and Field team throwing javelin. Our team went to Colorado Springs for a meet, and I was happy to hang out with my pal Colin. He was an incredible pole-vaulter, and the only one on our team who regularly medaled. We had a ball on the trip. He was a fun loving guy, and also happened to be my girlfriend Ammy's best friend. His vibrancy was matched by his mischief. We bought panties at a boutique from the hotel and hung them on the coaches' hotel doors. Upon our return from the meet (where he medaled, of course), he was practicing alone. He vaulted and missed the pad after his descent. He landed on the rubberized track and died from the impact to his head. His memorial was another lesson in mortality for me, and a sobering reminder of how precious my time with Dad was. Ammy would visit his parents every week that year, and I accompanied her a couple times to reminisce and remember my friend.

I think in the middle of my sophomore year, Dad had been given months to live. He told them to go to hell, that he had stuff he had to see. He wanted to see me graduate high school, and my sister Beck graduate Occupational Therapy school. Every few months they'd come back to him with a new deadline. He reiterated his desire for them to go to hell. Beck and I both graduated in May of 1995, and Dad died that August.

I'm not implying that there's something inherently heroic in going through a death. There can be, of course. But each of these deaths taught me not only of life's fragility and living it in each moment, but of carrying on through adversity. Letting each of these deaths empower you in a way; not necessarily allowing them to make you more fragile but harnessing them to reinforce the drive of living your life more heroically.

The drive that I have for legacy, to leave something tangible for my daughter presupposes that deeds don't live after us, that it's only the tangible things we leave behind that count. A tangible item is there, certainly, and can be called upon when left on a shelf as a book or a film. That can be a powerful thing (again, part of why I'm writing this) but a witnessed deed is far more powerful. That's my intended legacy to her; that through my actions, hopefully positive, she can learn something and have it stick with her. That's why kids remember their special teachers, and remember certain events.

Dad borrowed a camcorder to record my senior year, not trusting our memory of it. One of the things I'm most ashamed of in my entire life was the way I behaved on this tape. I played it so cool, so dickish. This was Dad's final document of how proud he was of his son. He followed me at javelin meets, award presentations, and every special moment. I acted as if I was embarrassed of the whole affair, and the man carried on despite my asshole behavior. I know my comeuppance is coming... up, and that's the nature of transitioning from childhood to adulthood. My heart will break a million times. I'm sure Dad's did, and that's on me. Every time I disobeyed, every lie (though there weren't many of those). Scottie will find that awful tape, perhaps, and see how atrocious Daddy was to her grandfather. Perhaps she'll learn another of those lessons I'm so fond of imparting.

As you've read in this book, we have such clear memories that can be triggered by a song, or a movie, or a place or a mood, memories that strike out of nowhere. That's important to hold onto. Again the deed supercedes the song or book that triggers the memory of the deed. That's our shared experience.

I recently watched one of those viral videos of a man in a nursing home, a man struggling with his faculties and almost entirely unresponsive to external stimuli. The introduction of music, specifically music from his era, lifted him in every sense (including literal). His love, his "geek-out" moment, manifested because of music. If I had a central thesis to this thing, it would be that **the term 'geek' is really just a synonym for _passion_.**

***

"To live is an awfully big adventure!"- Peter Pan

I'm glad Scottie has this book as a record, but hopefully this can serve as a launchpad/springboard for her to recall deeds that her mother and I did. Thus far, she's a beautiful human being. The compassion she exhibits when anyone is sick or hurt is extraordinary. When I ruptured my Achilles tendon (twice) she made every effort to take care of me, asking how my stomach felt and wanting to put dirt on my owie to fix it.

That's why, my friend. Why I felt such a need to write this book as some sort of tangible legacy. But legacy truly lives in our kids (yes 'our'- they're yours too). Mine's about to turn four, and traces of my legacy abound in her. For all the money, all the _stuff_ I give her… all I really want is to matter to her after I'm long gone. That story continues…

Epilogue: The more things change, the more they're different

2012 proved quite a change from when I first sat down to write this. Neither of us works for LPT anymore, as the theatre's financial difficulties forced us to migrate to other jobs. Colleen was hired as the Managing Director of another theatre company, and stayed there for nearly a year. This was also her most prolific year ever as a theatre artist (acting in one show, directing three, and choreographing five!)

While looking for supplemental work to the theatre, I was offered a full time position at the magnificent Mouse House. Yep, I'm at Disneyland four times a week as Jafar in *Aladdin: A Musical Spectacular*. I'm truly blessed and, as with every job, am performing like the gig could end tomorrow (and it could). Both of our new posts allowed us to give more time for Scottie and more time for a new... baby. Baby Loki.

When we found out we were pregnant in mid-2012, we wanted to get Scottie involved early. We asked her if she had any ideas on what to call the baby. Scottie considered for only a brief moment and replied "Loki. Baby Loki." We asked why she picked that one and Scottie rolled her eyes. "Loki is Fore's brova, Mama Dada." 'Fore' being Thor, of course. When we discovered we were having a girl, we asked Scottie if she wanted to amend the baby's name. Again, the eye roll and a simple "no." Fair enough.

We had to move out of our apartment and ended up encountering a fortunate situation that we had to act upon. The house directly behind Colleen's sister, brother-in-law, and nephew became available, and it fit all our criteria: close to Disney, an actual house, a bedroom for each of the girls, and a big back yard. Calm down- we're only renting. We can't afford to buy a home! We had a stairway leading up to a gate built, so the kids could go between the two yards whenever they liked. It's been great to hang with Renee, Dan, and AJ when I have time off. And I have a lawn to mow, when I actually get around to buying a lawnmower.

With Baby Loki in tow (now renamed Pepper Rae- 'Pepper' after Iron Man's Pepper Potts and 'Rae' after my Grandmother I never got to meet), we moved during my tech week of *Around the World in 80 Days*. I had taken a leave of absence from Disney to return to LPT and play one of my favorite literary characters, Phileas Fogg (or as Colleen called him, 'Phineas Ferb').

Colleen took the baby's birth as an opportunity to spend more time with the kids, so she left her position as Managing Director and now freelances as a Director/Choreographer/Actor/Artistic person. She's off to another prolific year in 2013, and I'm looking forward to her choreography for LPT's *Fiddler on the Roof*.

Scottie continues to triumph and, well, not triumph. She decided after over a year of potty training that she wanted to go on the big potty. Just like that. I made a big deal out of it and she looked at me as if to say "oh, this is what I do now- no biggie." I immediately went out and bought her Merida's outfit from *Brave* at the Disney Store. She can drink out of a cup, but prefers a bendy straw. But she's regressed back to needing her bobo fett for naps and bedtime, clearly negating all the "work" I did when I threw it out the window. And she's still not at ease with the beach, though a few trips yielded low tide wading (she held onto me for dear life).

Cinematically, 2012 may go down in history as one of the best times to be a geek. March saw *The Hunger Games* demolish the box office, and Hulk smashed through May in *Marvel's The Avengers*. This was the first Marvel film to be released as a Disney property, something that blows my mind (Disneyland is prepping a Stark Expo exhibit to coincide with the release of *Iron Man 3* this May). My pal Josh said it best when asked how he enjoyed *The Avengers*: "I want to give that movie a big hug." Colleen and I took the afternoon/evening to go to a luxury movie theatre in San Juan Capistrano, and my lovely bride (with whom I celebrated five years of marriage in September) bought tickets for the next showing in the middle of the New York battle scene. She returned with a beer (again, fancy-schmancy theatre) and informed me we'd be watching back-to-back showings. Attagirl. After the first show, we strolled through idyllic San Juan Capistrano and discussed the mythology of superheroes, and how Joss Whedon nailed the presentation of these archetypes while making the film fresh and accessible for both geeks and normies. I reminded her that everyone's a geek, and Colleen smiled. "Sure, honey. Sure."

The rest of the year brought us a revamped Spidey as portrayed by Andrew Garfield in Marc Webb's reboot *The Amazing Spider-Man*, the end of Christopher Nolan's epic Batman saga *The Dark Knight Rises*, Ridley Scott's return to the Alien universe in *Prometheus*, a new James Bond adventure in *Skyfall*, and even history geeks had their day with Steven Spielberg's Daniel Day-Lewis starrer *Lincoln*. One of the most welcome excursions for me was my journey back into Middle Earth with Peter Jackson's *The Hobbit* (Part one of three!). 80s nostalgia came back briefly in the film *Rock of Ages*, itself an adaptation of the stage musical featuring power ballads and rock anthems from the likes of Styx, Journey, and Poison. I, uh, didn't see this film.

2012 also marked the 20th anniversary of Image Comics, the 50th anniversary of Marvel Superheroes (The Fantastic Four and the Hulk in '62), and the 25th anniversary of the ultra-violent and amazing *Robocop*. Geeks rejoiced, and will continue to do so now that Joss

Whedon has made superheroes ubiquitous. Here's hoping his low-budget adaptation of *Much Ado About Nothing* does the same for Shakespeare.

Disney furnished gigantic geek news once again at the tail end of 2012. They announced not only the purchase of Lucasfilm, but also that new Star Wars films would be coming as early as 2015. And the first one was to be directed by wunder-geek J.J. Abrams (responsible for bridging the geek/norm gap with his re-imagined *Star Trek* in 2009).

From family to career, 2012 proved a year filled with transition and triumph. When it all comes down to it, I'm Joe: pre-volcano, on his raft of designer luggage, staring up at a moon so full that both it and its reflection on the inky ocean waves eclipse the night sky itself, and thanking God for my life. Despite the fact that I live in perpetual fear (kidding, mostly), I'm grateful to find the spirit of adventure in everyday life. To quote/paraphrase Carl Denham in *King Kong*: "there is so little wonder left in the world, so little true adventure." When I hear of a new species of sea life discovered, or even the possibility of an alien vessel unearthed on the ocean floor, I get giddy. I start to imagine, and my mind churns restlessly to figure out the answers to the universe. We know so much about so many things. Perhaps Scottie's generation will look inward, taking a *Fantastic Voyage* through *Innerspace*. Or perhaps the next frontier is a digital one, as Kevin Flynn predicted in *TRON*. Whatever it is, I'll discover it with/through Scottie and Pepper.

When watching *Explorers* with Scottie, she echoes the sense of wonder and awe of rocketing toward the stars that I felt at her age. Now four and a half, she sits with me on our front lawn manipulating the brilliant *Star Walk* app on my phone. We look up at the stars and identify constellations. Hercules is her favorite, though "da bear one" is slowly creeping up to a close second. "What are dey doing up dere, Daddy?" "What are *who* doing up dere?" I ask. She corrects herself. "Up *there*. What are the stars doing up there?" I ponder the question. So many ways to answer. I'd normally try to reverse it and ask, "What do *you* think they're doing?" She lifts the iphone to identify some stars and points to the brightest one in the Hercules Constellation. "That star, my little weewok? That star, all of them actually, are telling us their final stories before they flash out of existence."

She looks up into the great beyond, not really understanding. "I don't think that's pretty good. But I like their stories. Let's just listen, Daddy." And in our front yard, on the top of a hill in Oceanside California, we listen.

Acknowledgments

To Scott Damian, Noel Douglas Orput, and Dylan White. All writers, all incredibly supportive of this project, and great friends to boot.

To all of Scottie's sitters, friends and family, who have given their time and love to care for our weewok.

To Minga and Grumps, the incredible in-laws.

To Digby Wolfe for his instruction and counsel, in academia and in life.

To Rosie, for treating me like another son, and for teaching me my colors.

To my siblings on both sides: Mark, Deb, Beck, Trampas, and Trever. Thanks for all the pillow fights, video game sessions, sporting endeavors, and roughhousing.

To Mom and Pops, for being incredible parents and continuing to persevere through my career choice.

To Colleen. Not only did you marry this schmuck, but you gave him two beautiful daughters.

And finally to my father, Manny Smith, for insisting I write, write, write...

About the Author

Lance Arthur Smith received his BA in Theatre with concentrations in Writing and Acting at the University of New Mexico under the tutelage of Emmy-winning writer Digby Wolfe (co-creator of *Laugh-In*). He has written for the stage, television, and film. *Princess Geek* is his first book.

Lance lives in Oceanside, California with his wife and two daughters. They have a garden with watermelon that refuses to grow, but a nifty grassy stretch for the Slip n' Slide.

You can follow him on Twitter at his handle @LanceArthur or read his award-winning blog *When the Power Goes Out* at http://www.sandiegoreader.com/weblogs/when-the-power-goes-out/

www.ingramcontent.com/pod-product-compliance
Lightning Source LLC
Chambersburg PA
CBHW022104280326
41933CB00007B/257